CROSS-COUNTRY SKIING

A COMPLETE GUIDE
BY
BRIAN CAZENEUVE

Illustrations by Ron Hildebrand

A TRAILSIDE SERIES GUIDE

W. W. NORTON & COMPANY

NEW YORK   LONDON

Look for these other Trailside® Series Guides:

Bicycling: Touring and Mountain Bike Basics
Hiking & Backpacking: A Complete Guide
Kayaking: Whitewater and Touring Basics
Winter Adventure: A Complete Guide to Winter Sports

Trailside is a registered trademark of New Media, Inc.

First Edition

The text of this book is composed in Bodoni Book with the display set in Triplex
Page composition by LaserImage
Color separations and prepress by Bergman Graphics, Incorporated

Illustrations by Ron Hildebrand

Book design by Bill Harvey

Library of Congress Cataloging-in-Publication Data

Cazeneuve, Brian, 1965–
Cross-country skiing: a complete guide/ by Brian Cazeneuve;
illustrations by Ron Hildebrand.
p. cm. — (A trailside series guide)
Includes bibliographical references and index.
1. Cross-country skiing. I. Title. II. Series.
GV855.3.C39 1995   795.932–dc20   95-5529

ISBN 0-393-31335-2

W. W. Norton & Company, Inc., 500 Fifth Avenue, New York, NY 10110
W. W. Norton & Company Ltd., 10 Coptic Street, London WC1A 1PU

2 3 4 5 6 7 8 9 0

INDEX

CONTENTS

NORDIC ORIGINS

Winter had just peeked around autumn's corner one morning on the peaceful trails of West Yellowstone, Montana, where visitors came to watch bison and bald eagles, not Nordic skiers. The altitude, 6,000 feet above sea level, made breathing something you had to think about.

Here, Nikolai Anikin, 1956 Olympic champion from the Russian factory city of Voskresensk, was standing facing two sets of neatly groomed parallel tracks that seemed to run about the same. Only the earnest and obliging teacher, visiting America on a coaching exchange, could feel the winds of urgency and amusement blowing side by side on those tracks.

Passing by on the left, hastened John, a man wearing U.S.A. national team colors and shaped like an oak tree. Arms and legs, instruments of his trade, were tuned to exquisite pitch and moved in fluid verse. There was no idle motion, no pause to dislodge the icicle weighting his chin.

Anikin's fractured English shook the mountains. "And zee pushing. Harder! Edge eez cutting. Compress! Hand eez high. Tail eez in zee track. Full the striding! Fighting harder! And zee pushing."

Anikin let his protégé loose and spun to face the right lane. Then he smiled. "Jo-le-ne. . . " he said,

proudly extending the name an extra note. "Eez guuuud."

Jolene bounded with a skip to her step, which could turn to a slide at a moment's imbalance. Her limbs moved with little semblance of sync as her knees and elbows persuaded the other parts to follow. This was her first time on the trails, and the way Anikin saw it, intent could atone for lack of skill any day.

Deliberately within his pupil's view, his hands feathered the air like a stretching harpsichordist's and his

singsong syllables played in pairs. "So nice, Jo-le-ne. And gliding on one leg. Little hill — take like baby. Slow rise. Good, soft. And gliding on one leg."

Anikin's call to calm nestled Jolene into her stride. The improvements were unmistakable and her grin was as grand as the canyon. "Only half an hour, Jo-le-ne? Eez

SAVE THE KING

Skiing prowess preserved the Norwegian monarchy in 1206, when civil war ravaged the empire. Prince Haakon Haakonsson was only two and would have fallen into enemy hands had it not been for two especially fleet-of-ski Birkebeiners ("Birchlegs"), so called because members of the insurgent Viking group who couldn't afford shoes instead bound animal skins around their legs with strips of birch bark in order to minimize moisture in their moccasins.

The Birkebeiners outskied their pursuers by fleeing eastward across the mountains from Lillehammer to Rena. Raised in Trondheim under soldiers' protection, Haakon claimed his throne at age 18 and reigned until 1263 as medieval Norway's most esteemed ruler.

Today the flight of the Birkebeiners is recalled by the medieval skier on Lillehammer's coat of arms, and the biennial Birkebeiner ski race over the original route of the rescue commemorates the event. Competitors carry 5.5-kilogram backpacks for 57 kilometers that include a cumulative ascent of 600 meters. The weary finisher will cross the finish line in a princely three hours, with stragglers to follow in as many as six.

Birkebeiner marathoners also populate the American Midwest, but generally skip the backpacks on race day.

> 66 Although skiing had spread, it was a national sport only in Norway. The forms of competition were often invented on the spot. A challenge would be issued and accepted. It might be to take off one's vest between the top and bottom of a given hill, or carry a full mug of beer to the bottom without spilling a single drop. 99

—Jakob Vaage,
ski historian

wonderful!"

Jolene looked like a five-year-old stumbling into a lollipop store. In fact, she was a normal, active twenty-something-year-old — but as easily could have been an eighty-something-year-old — whose childlike sense of discovery was rekindled by the delight of cross-country skiing.

FOR EVERYONE

Cross-country skiing, unlike hang gliding, cattle rustling, and iambic Swahili, is disproportionately more difficult to perfect than it is

to learn. It is as elegant and simple as the sight of snowflakes; as distinct and precise as the shape of snowflakes.

It rewards the outdoorsman with nonpareil scenes of august mountains and intoxicating scents of fir trees, all the while leaving Mother Earth unaware of the slashing and schussing just inches above her belly.

It pacifies the urbanite who generally fancies snow as little more than slush fodder on his daily clump to the office. Give him a weekend trail and suddenly taxes are forgotten, faxes are forbidden, and the harmonic accord with nature cleanses remnants of last Friday's 9:00-to-5:00 turned 7:30-to-midnight workday as though it never happened.

The low-impact, heart-pumping invigoration is the perfect way to get away from life, though in Nordic lands it is the centuries-old way of life. It can become a way of life for you too.

Norwegian Ancestry

The word "ski" comes from the Norwegian *skith* meaning

For centuries the primary mode of winter transportation in Scandinavia, there remains something deeply satisfying about speeding across snow-covered terrain on skinny skis, even in the machine-set tracks of the Nordic center.

either "snowshoe" or "strip of wood," transport's building block of choice before the age of shock absorbers. Late in the 19th century archaeologists unearthed a rock carving on a cave wall in Rodoy, a town in the county of Nordland located near the Arctic Circle. The carving, a stick-figure depiction of a skier using a single bent pole for balance, is the earliest visual evidence of the activity on record. The skis appear nearly twice the size of the traveler, who seems to have rabbit ears attached to his head, though not for good luck. The man was probably a hunter, his headdress intended to fool unsuspecting — and very naive — prey into thinking he was just cousin Bugs out for a stroll.

Wooden skis preserved in the moss bogs of northern Sweden date

as far back as 3000 B.C. Some of the world's oldest skis are displayed at the Fjiugarden Museum of Sweden. Recent cultural studies attribute skiing's origins to the Sami, the indigenous people of Norway, whose contribution to mainstream culture has been overlooked through the centuries. Motifs on Sami drums depict men hunting on skis — and even competing against each other — as far back as 5000 B.C., when the Sami dialect, containing over a dozen traditional words linked to skiing, first flourished.

Other motifs reveal Sami hunters being towed on skis by reindeer, and Sami writings indicate the first ski competitions may actually have been reindeer races with prizes awarded the victorious driver's family and village. "The Sami people were so proficient on skis," the 12th-century Icelandic saga writer Snorri Sturluson wrote, "that even the animals could not outdistance them." Norse

SCOTT VS. AMUNDSEN

Roald Amundsen's zest for expedition began at 22, when a planned 72-mile hike from Oslo to Bergen went hopelessly wrong. Encircled by blizzard conditions, Amundsen and his partner were trapped for four days after exhausting their food supply. Once rescued, Amundsen decided he'd had so much fun he'd make it a career.

By 1910, despite deepening debt, Amundsen had mustered the necessary financial backing for a journey to the North Pole. But while planning the trip, he learned erroneously that two navigators had preceded him there. "Why should anyone want to go to a place where someone else has been?" Amundsen later wrote.

For more than a year he planned in secret to go instead to the South Pole, saving the minor detail of his destination for some members of his traveling troupe until after sea navigation began. At the time, Robert F. Scott, a competitive British colonel, was also sailing southward, and Amundsen infused a sense of destiny (and confidence) in his men by telling them they were racing against the British.

Later, traveling the Arctic by dogsled and skis, Amundsen wrote in his diary, "Cannot understand what the English mean when they say dogs cannot be used here." The frostbitten Brits had also proclaimed the uselessness of fur clothes before the trip on which several subsequently froze to death. What's more, their sleds were too heavy, their food supply

Heading off through deep powder into the backcountry of the Colorado Rockies. What other sport offers such ready access to adventure?

was too paltry, and their capacity to misread the locations of their own depots was mystifying.

Amundsen employed 97 dogs and a team of expert skiers to guide him to the pole, which he reached successfully on December 14. His team included Olav Bjaaland, a renowned Holmenkollen ski champion, ski maker, and carpenter, who, on skis, boldly led the returning sleds through the darkened wilderness.

Amundsen successfully negotiated the so-called Devil's Ballroom, where his mates tiptoed about random crevasses on ice that threatened them with its frightening crackles. Throughout the trip, they used the meat of the dogs who couldn't pull their weight to fill the stomachs of those who could.

When he lodged in a Tasmanian hotel upon his return, Amundsen, appearing as tattered as his attire, was given what he called "the tramp's room," from which he exchanged cables with his king.

Ever the bumbler, Scott reached the pole a month after Amundsen, and had nearly completed his return when his supplies ran out. His body was later found less than 15 miles from its destination.

?

During the 1994 Lillehammer Winter Olympic Games, natives were uncharacteristically aghast at organizers' wishes to restrain spectators from camping near the course for cross-country events that finished at Birkebeiner Stadium. Norwegian law, after all, had long permitted skiers to traverse public lands — even to stop for a nap — without objection.

The flap fizzled and campers who slumbered in subzero frost were among the nearly 200,000 — in a nation of just 4 million — spectators who hollered their daily encouragement to the skiers. Still others perched on rooftops or laid squatters' rights to tree branches they had climbed during moonlight hours.

Along the course, the low, steady rumble of hand-shaken cowbells rode the racers through the finish, where King Harald V saluted medalist and also-ran alike with his own cowbell shake.

mythology also refers to Skade, the Ski Goddess, and Ull, the Ski God.

For the commoner, skis were the only practical mode of transportation and, ultimately, a necessity for survival. To tend livestock, barter at market, or visit Aunt Ingrid, villagers were compelled to ski. Doctors and midwives traveled with medicines on skis. Bride and groom often skied to their wedding; a sopping bridal gown was a sure sign of faulty technique. Since churches in Scandinavia were usually built on a hill, Sunday school was a joy for children, who could look forward to the downhill slopes once the Bible was closed.

Skis were especially essential for food gathering. One Viking legend has the king telling his son that his troop of soldiers could "strike nine reindeer with their spears, and many more after that" while still maintaining stride. The strikes were likely made with ski poles whose tips had been sharpened for harpooning.

Military Traditions

By 1500, expert skimanship was required of every member of the Swedish army. Border guards operated on skis during the winter, when most military campaigns took place, since the short farming season was no time for hostilities.

Young cross-country soldiers were on the front lines of the Great Scandinavian War of 1700-1718, and years later, in 1767, a retired general may have hatched the world's first

The 1994 Lillehammer Winter Olympic Games, where 200,000 Norwegians lined the cross-country course to cheer on competitors in their national sport.

THE HOLMENKOLLEN

Norwegians will tell you they have two national days: Constitution Day on May 17, and Hol-menkollen Sunday in early March. The later is the finale to the annual 11-day ski festival that celebrates the soul of Norwegian culture. Think of a dawn-to-dusk, family-suitable Mardi Gras where the ice is kicking up underfoot rather than swimming in some rapscallion's gin fizz.

The revelry began in 1892 with a one-day competition as an answer to the jumping and skiing festivals in Huseby that had drawn over 10,000 spectators.

King Olav V made his debut as a Holmenkollen jumper in 1922, and the facility sports a life-size statue of His Majesty with a rucksack on his back and his dog at his side traipsing through the Norwegian forests.

Within Telemarking distance sits the world's first ski museum, carved from bedrock in the shadow of the enormous ski jump

continued on next page

and completed in 1926. It includes the wooden skis that Roald Amundsen used to reach the South Pole in 1912 and the well-preserved, chunky remains of a ski excavated from two centuries of being "bogged down" in Sweden. Other exhibits include an ancient 11-foot-long pair of skis from Oppland and a country ski maker's shop where visitors drop their jaws at the sight of an over-alled craftsman sitting on a stool with hammers, glue pots, and wooden strips on his left and finished skis on his right.

For years, the ode to culture was also an affirmation of manhood. Women were believed too brittle to be among Bunyanesque mountain men and were excluded from the Holmenkollen competitions until alpine events were introduced in 1947. A cross-country race was finally created for women in 1954. It covered 10 kilometers and included two disqualifications for "bodily harmful interference." Mrs. Bunyan, perhaps.

Today's festival includes cross-country races for disabled skiers, age-group contests for every classification from toddlers to grandfathers, biathlon and other military-related events, and even a race for members of the Scandinavian parliament in which participants are heartily cheered. Would that happen in a Congressional marathon?

biathlon event when he suggested a diversion for officers in ski-runner companies at the Norwegian-Swedish border. The contest offered 20 Riksdollars, almost a week's wage, to the officer who could run the course and hit still targets at 30, 40, and 50 paces with his rifle.

In the mid-19th century, the primary proponents of skiing were rifle clubs. The world's first known ski organization, the Tyrsil Rifle and Ski Club, was formed in 1861 to encourage national defense.

At the same time, Scandinavian settlers were introducing skiing to the northern United States. In 1856, Norse expatriate Jon Torsteinson Rui ("Snowshoe Thompson") began carrying mail across the Sierra Nevada on his skis. For 20 years Thompson's was the only winter route available in the area, and his postal recompense was said to include frequent samplings of spirits.

Two brothers from Thompson's home region of Telemark, Mikkel and Torjus Hemmestveit, were the first to

charge admission and entry fees for a series of touring races in the Midwestern states during the 1880s. The brothers also proposed the creation of a national governing body for skiing, which was finally founded in 1905 as the National Ski Association. In 1962, the NSA became the U.S. Ski Association, which is now the sport's governing body.

■

Many people are apt to see lift lines and resorts when they picture skiing. Alpiners may be distant descendants of the hunting stick figure, but perhaps owing to man's need to speed, to flaunt, downhill skiing has won over much of the common consciousness in relatively short order. Americans

Biathlon, a mix of Nordic racing and marksmanship, grew out of Scandinavia's history of fighting its wars on skis.

?

DID YOU KNOW

Cross-country's competitive side has given rise to other more casual diversions. Biathlon, introduced in the 1960 Squaw Valley Games, is a skiing-and-shooting replication of medieval military defense. It tests the uneasy marriage of a racing heart rate and a steady hand. These days the forfeit for a missed target is a penalty loop, and only the pride is wounded.

who wouldn't know Bill Koch from Diet Coke (pronounce the skier like the soft drink) are quite aware of Jean-Claude Killy's savoir faire and Tommy Moe's come-from-nowhere Olympic victory. Can you name any Nordic Olympic medalist?

Unlike cross-country with its time-proven utility, alpine skiing developed primarily as a function of Evel Knievel hormones gone tipsy. It also spawned snowboarding, a growing sport for surfers who got lost on their way to the beach, but had fun anyway.

Ski mind-sets often vary with the terrain, and the alpine lift line can be a theater of shameless revisionism. The Nordic ski tourer doesn't care. If she Telemarked into a bush an hour ago, she'll tell you — and warn you

The world of cross-country skiing is unbounded by manmade resorts. It is as vast as the great outdoors in winter and your own imagination and ability.

66 Facing the hut, I could see the Grunhorn-Lucke, which we had crossed from the Concordia, the soft shimmer of its moonlit snows penciled by the pattern of our ski tracks, the snow thrown up by swings showing like the delicate burr of a silver point etching. Seldom have I known a happiness so unquestioning and so complete. 99

—Sir Arnold Lunn,
ski journalist and commentator

to watch for the turn. The delightful anomaly of ski touring is the typical cross-country thoroughfare, where you might notice, say, three hearty souls on your trail — until you face-plant and six people suddenly stop to help you up.

Cross-country skiing's possibilities are endless. The landscape of your imagination is gloriously unbounded by hill bottoms, unclut-tered by acrobatics, and unmitigated by chairlifts and base lodges.

With ample room for excellence and folly, the cross-country trail is open to everyone.

GEARING
UP

One of the many wonders of cross-country skiing is that, relative to many other sports, gearing up is really more a matter of gearing down. Few other sports require so little or such straightforward, reasonably priced gear. When you add to the equation the superb aerobic workout you'll gain along with the sheer pleasure, the result is hard to beat. Still, there are decisions to be made.

TO RENT. . .

Your first ski purchase is making you a little antsy. One foot inside the ski shop and you've just crossed the fault line. You slink unobtrusively toward the 20-foot-long wall of skis on display, careful to avoid setting off a "Can I help you?" from a salesman before you're ready. But when it comes, the question puts you off balance just the same.

The words leave your mouth without warning, and your glassy stare reeks of cluelessness. I, um, like the green ones. Oh, sure, now you've done it. You're doomed to purchase something no better than barrel staves, or else an exquisitely engineered pair, that will perform superbly in every type of skiing you're not planning to try. But the, um, green looks pretty cool.

Relax. Several pointers will ease

High-top skating boots for extra ankle support. Selecting the right boot/binding system is the key to comfort and performance.

aid of a qualified instructor to fit you properly in rented boots, skis, and poles and then show you how to use them, you will grasp more than you imagined in less time than you thought possible. Still, it may take you four or five outings on rented equipment before you're ready to make a purchase; take your time. Try as many types of skiing as you can and become familiar with different equipment. Seek advice, being as specific as possible about your particular aims. Then experiment some more and ask more questions. Now you are ready to stop in at a ski shop that specializes in cross-country gear; don't bother with general sporting goods dealers or those ski shops that concentrate on downhill equipment, giving only halfhearted attention to Nordic gear.

your angst. First, don't be intimidated. You are skiing for fun; you're not using skis as a means of subsistence transport. Second, ski sales people are generally far more helpful, knowledgeable, and scrupulous than car dealers and won't — or shouldn't — be offended or conniving if you are ignorant about their products. Third — and this is most important — don't even contemplate buying equipment when you're so green that you are in danger of embarrassing yourself. Rent gear and try it out before you buy. Many ski shops and all reputable ski touring centers rent skis, poles, and boots. Such a touring center is the place to get acquainted with cross-country skiing. With the

. . .OR TO BUY

Your skis, bindings, and boots should reflect your expectations — no matter how modest or ambitious — based on time spent on rented or borrowed skis. Do you fancy ventures into uncharted backcountry terrain as a complement to the backpacking you do in the warmer months, regular cardiovascular workouts around the local Nordic center track, or ski weekends away from your workaday urban world? Your answers will give a qualified salesperson clues to the sort of gear you'll need for your journey.

Avoid mass merchandisers who may not be able to answer your questions. Go to a ski shop or outfitter that specializes in Nordic equipment. Salespeople in those shops are probably the most enthusiastic skiers you will find. They care about the sport and are eager to infect you with their enthusiasm by giving you the wherewithal to learn about it and enjoy it. They will also be happy to advise you about local trails, touring centers, and conditions.

While cross-country gear is reasonably priced, it's wise to become familiar with equipment options by renting or borrowing as you learn the sport.

TEST RUNS. Find out when ski companies or ski shops are holding "demo days" in your area, usually in early winter. You can test-drive virtually any piece of equipment on one of these days, and company reps will be on hand to answer your queries. Using two slightly different skis, boots, or poles from the same family at the same time is one way to assess how your body will respond to certain subtle variations in design. Make

sure a test run includes the turns, flats, and ups and downs you're likely to encounter once you have actually made a purchase.

At first, you may do well to ask for a combination ski that is versatile enough to use in different conditions for different types of skiing. Once you become more experienced and competent enough to appreciate the benefits of specialized equipment for certain types of skiing, you may wish to trade up. ON SALE. Be on the lookout for fall ski sales and exchanges where you can pick up very inexpensive used gear. Such exchanges are especially valuable for families outfitting growing children; you can buy used gear one year, then sell it back the following season and purchase all new used gear to keep up

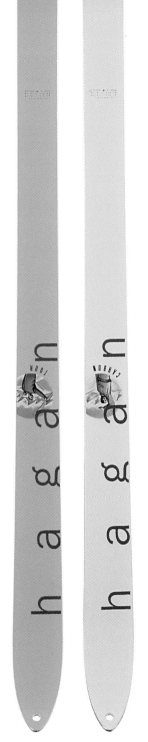

These Hagan skis are specially designed for deep powder mountaineering skiing. They are wide overall, have pronounced side cut, and wide shovels (see pages 29-30).

with your growing child. These sales are often sponsored by ski clubs, so there are knowledgeable, helpful people on the floor to assist you. Arrive early.

MATCHING EQUIPMENT. Just as a Phillips screwdriver won't work with a slotted screw, certain ski gear will not work with other ski gear. Ask the salesperson to help you and make sure that your skis are compatible with your boot/binding system. If you buy boots and bindings separately, be sure they match. A New Nordic Norm (NNN) binding won't bind itself to a three-pin boot.

A glance at a couple's equipment can tell you that he plans to kick and glide, while she plans to skate. The recent specialization of cross-country gear is that telling. It may have been easier in the days when everyone held bamboo poles, wore a wool sweater, strapped on wooden skis with cable bindings, and routinely double-poled from here to there. But

today there are more equipment options and therefore more skiing options. When you buy a piece of equipment, you should be aware of its capacities and limitations. If learning all of this seems daunting, be assured that the effort will ultimately leave you better equipped to ski better.

SKIS

Since snow is the base of necessity, different snow characteristics determine the type of equipment you use. Some skis are waxable; others are waxless. Some are called fat boys; others are micro skis. Some are made for turns; others simply make tracks. Some like it hot; others prefer powder or ice or crud. Essentially, though, all cross-country skis fall into one of four categories: classical skis, skating skis, combination skis, and backcountry skis. Each style performs optimally in certain conditions, though some skis are quite versatile.

THE MODERN SKI IS BORN

By at least one criterion, Sondre Norheim began skiing's "modern" era over a century ago. If, in fact, skiing has been around for as many as 7,000 years, it didn't become an accessible amusement until Thomas Edison's Norwegian predecessor began tinkering with its particulars.

Born in Telemark, a sleepy village in the Morgedal Valley, in 1825, Norheim made three significant contributions to skiing that have stood the test of innovation.

For thousands of years, ski practitioners — particularly hunters and tradesmen — used two skis of different lengths: a primary gliding ski that could be as long as 10 feet, and a shorter skating ski used to propel oneself forward. This shorter ski was often covered in animal fur, a forerunner of today's kick wax and climbing skins, allowing the skier to proceed smoothly in a forward direction, while resisting any slack in the opposite direction. This was especially helpful for skiers who needed to climb hills.

Norheim developed what he called "waisted" skis — sturdy wooden models of equal length and purpose. He refined the idea constantly until 1870, when he finally produced the Telemark ski, a model that was narrower in the middle and wider at the tail and tip, the first skis that had what we now call a side cut.

To go with his later ski
continued on next page

THE MODERN SKI IS BORN
continued from previous page

models, Norheim developed a stiff heel binding made of birch root that simplified both jumping and downhill turning. The new binding replaced the underfoot leather strap that twirled about the toe and tended either to loosen spontaneously or simply break after a good tug. Norheim was a shameless showman who leaped from roofs and performed a varied array of stunts at carnivals. having secured foot to ski, Norheim was no longer forced to keep ski on snow. At 42, nearly twice the age of his challengers, he won numerous skiing and jumping contests that gave rise to today's Olympic Nordic combined.

Fifty centuries is a long time to figure out how to turn. Using an equivalent timeline, imagine what our highways would still look like. Norheim's new skis allowed him greater freedom of movement. On bent knee, he mastered turns that he began popularizing at various ski festivals throughout the countryside, most notably the hillside site at Huseby that gave rise to the Holmenkollen Festival years later. Over time, cross-country skiers employed other turns besides Norheim's famous Telemark turn, which became the cornerstone of downhilling in future years. In the early 1970s, backcountry loyalists rediscovered the trusty Telemark in the Rocky Mountains and reincorporated the maneuver into the skiing mainstream.

SNOW SURFACES

The prepared trails at a Nordic center give you a consistent, packed surface and set tracks, a pair of grooves set in the snow just the right distance apart so that you can stride out like a train on its track. On such groomed trails, you want narrow skis designed to follow a track more easily and let you stride out. Wider skis are designed to take you far from the set tracks of the Nordic center. They "float" on deep powder, and their increased surface area provides firmer footing on crud and chopped ice. Such skis let you adjust to unpredictable backcountry conditions and challenging terrain, and are more akin to downhill skis in that they let you cut turns in the snow.

Ski Characteristics

CAMBER. Lay a ski flat on the floor. Notice that the tip and tail touch the floor, but there is a long bowlike arc in the body of the ski that does not. This raised portion is the ski's camber, and the amount of camber

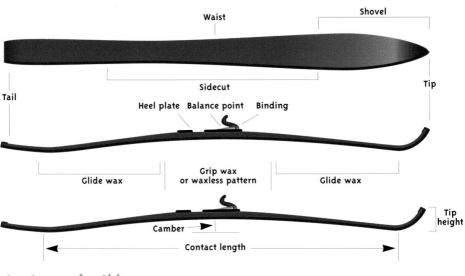

Waist

Shovel

Sidecut

Tail

Tip

Heel plate   Balance point   Binding

Glide wax

Grip wax
or waxless pattern

Glide wax

Tip
height

Camber

Contact length

Anatomy of a Ski

Subtle variations in the profile of skis (the amount of side cut, the width of their shovel, the degree of camber) coupled with their overall length, width, and stiffness profoundly affect how they behave on snow. Long, narrow, straight, stiff skis are made for going fast straight ahead in set tracks. Short, wide skis with more side cut, wider shovels, and more flex are made for cutting turns.

determines how much force you'll need to apply to bring the midsection in contact with the snow during your kick. Heavier skiers and those with more experience and assertive technique will want a ski with more camber. Lighter skiers and those with a less aggressive kick will want a softer camber in order to grip the snow with less effort. Skis with too much camber can be tiring to use: they are difficult to turn and can slip backward when climbing uphill. Skis with less camber are easier to turn, though they don't glide nearly as straight or as well.

The camber is also the wax pocket on which you will apply a grip wax (or where the waxless pattern is

molded into the ski bottom), an essential if you're inclined to climb the incline. Touring skis need more camber than Telemark models because when you are gliding rather than climbing, you don't want much contact between the grip wax (or the waxless pattern) and the snow (see above). Telemark skiers who want to have fun cutting downhill turns don't need a ski with much camber; they need the full length of the ski on the snow to turn with ease, and they are likely to use skins rather than grip wax on long climbs.

Racing skis, the narrowest, lightest skis available, have the greatest (and stiffest) camber, to reduce drag by keeping as much of

the ski off the snow as possible.

FLEX. A ski's flexibility also influences its turning characteristics and can tell you what to expect when you want to change direction. Just as you want your car's steering mechanism to work properly, you want to be comfortable with your ski's flex. As a test, with the ski's tail planted on the floor and its base side facing away from you, pull the ski tip toward you while pushing the belly in the opposite direction — as though you were about to fling some slush off the ski tip and into somebody's face. Try this with several different models in order to compare the difference among ski models.

Then grab the ski's belly with one hand and with the other hand twist the tip as though you were opening a jar of mustard. A rigid tip will serve you well in packed snow and ice when you don't want any accidental turns. If, however, you're the type who sees the turn coming at the touring center and braces for the impending face-plant, a more forgiving torque will allow you to negotiate the curves of groomed trails with machine-set tracks.

In general, stiff skis ride straighter, while softer skis act as shock absorbers that handle uneven terrain and float well in power snow.

SIDE CUT. Viewed from above, skis with side cut have an hourglass figure. They are wider toward the tip

---

TECHNIQUE TIP

THE PAPER TEST

Before buying new skis, learn whether they have the right degree of camber for your weight by employing the unscientific but reliable paper test. With the skis set side by side on the floor of the ski shop, stand on them where the bindings would be. While you are comfortably balanced on them, ask a friend to slide a piece of paper under the midsection of each ski. The paper should slide relatively freely under a 2½-foot-long section of the ski beneath your feet. If the paper is pinned to the floor, the skis' camber is too soft for your weight, and too much of its base will be in constant contact with the snow, slowing your glide. If the paper slides freely beneath more than around 2½ feet, the camber is too stiff for your weight, and you'll have difficulty producing enough downward force for the skis to grip the snow when you're kicking or going uphill.

For the somewhat obsessed, the paper test also allows you to locate and mark the wax pocket on your pair of skis so you know exactly where to apply grip wax.

and tail than in the middle, or waist, and the difference between the measurements is called the side cut. A larger side cut facilitates turning, since it allows the ski to move more quickly from edge to edge. A smaller side cut facilitates straight-line travel. Look for a slim waist if you plan to turn frequently; a straight and even ski will help you stride the straight and narrow path more efficiently.

Models that are straight from tip to tail have what is called a "parallel cut" and are often used by racers who simply want to go fast. In set tracks, the parallel cut reduces friction. Telemark skis, like downhill skis, have greater side cut.

Types of Skis

TOURING (CLASSICAL). Regular touring skis are reasonably wide and stable. These skis will perform fine in set tracks, but unlike light touring skis, they are also useful if you decide to break your own trail away from the Nordic center, since the added surface area gives you more control and flotation on deeper snow. Touring skis are usually matched to the relatively wide 75 mm, three-pin boot/bindings (see page 31). With these skis you can go touring at a park, a forest, even your local golf course, but also enjoy a spin around the Nordic center's machine-set tracks.

LIGHT TOURING (CLASSICAL). The most basic form of track skiing — also called light touring — employs lightweight skis that are narrower and have more camber, livelier flex, and less side cut than touring skis for top performance in set tracks. Light touring models are invariably matched to one of the boot/binding systems (see page 32). They are underachievers, however, away from groomed trails.

SKATING. "Skating ski" appears to be a misnomer the likes of "jumbo shrimp," yet this latest evolution of the cross-country ski is winning many converts who value a truly strenuous aerobic workout.

Perhaps the most specialized

Rossignol ski construction. Different wood-laminate cores make for different skiing characteristics. (Top) Touring ski, with a wood/air core that reduces weight; (middle) a lightweight Compact Series ski, with a vertical laminated wood core surrounded by a fiberglass bias ply torsion box for rigidity; and (bottom) a Telemark ski, with a solid laminated wood core surrounded by a full fiberglass torsion box.

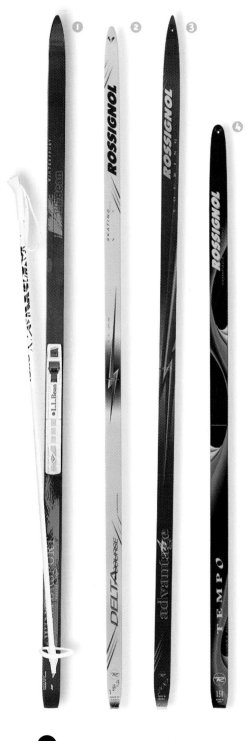

skis on the market (they even require specialized high-top boots), skating models evolved from racing skis as the skating stride began to replace the diagonal stride among cross-country racers. Light, short, narrow, and with very stiff camber, they are designed to operate gracefully on groomed, firm snow. Because skating skis are meant to be edged (that is, pushed off on an angle), they are rigid and averse to conventional turning, and they don't work at all well in soft snow. Skating in deep powder is like pushing off against Jell-O: several thrusts and you're still stuck in the same place. The more packed the snow, the more easily you'll be able to push off.

Yet skating skis are so short that they are very maneuverable. It used to be that skis were always longer than ski poles. These days skis are getting shorter and poles are getting longer for virtually all skiers, but especially for skaters, who now use shorter skis than poles. Early skating models were only 10 to 15 cm shorter than light touring models, but recently introduced micro skis come as short as 140 cm and as narrow as 42 mm. Once you find a comfortable

1-2) **Classic Touring:** Designed primarily for track skiing, but with just enough width, side cut (about 3 mm), and flex for breaking trails and turning.
3) **Racing/Skating:** A shorter, narrower ski with almost no side cut and blunt tip typical of skating skis. For groomed trails only.
4) **Skating:** Wider than the racing/skating model, this would be a good first skating ski.

pair of skating skis — and a comfortable stride to go with them — you
are on your way to having as pleasurable an aerobic workout as you'll find
with any activity.

COMBINATION. What if you want to
have your skate and still enjoy the
occasional detour? Designers have
come up with hybrid models. Essentially, a combination ski takes the
dimensions and characteristics of
skating skis and touring skis and
splits the difference between them.
"Combi skis" are the jacks of all
trades and may be the ideal first purchase for a beginner. But to master
one of the trades, you're better off
using other skis that are labor-spe-
cific. If you find yourself skiing more
than once a month and become experienced enough to know you prefer
certain types of skiing over others,
you will probably want to graduate
from a single pair of combi skis to an
additional pair or pairs that better
suit your favorite sport.

BACKCOUNTRY TOURING AND
MOUNTAINEERING. Most modern

1) Telemark (powder): A short ski with extra
wide shovel and ample side cut (20 mm) for
controlled turns in deep, steep powder.
2) Telemark (packed powder): A longer, stiffer
Telemark model designed to handle the packed
snow at downhill areas.
3) Mountaineering: This ski has plenty of side
cut (13 mm) and is wide enough for good
downhill performance, but is narrower and has
a less pronounced shovel than the Telemark skis.
It would be good for hut-to-hut treks where
touring is combined with downhill runs.
4) Racing: In contrast, this classic racing model
has no side cut and is very narrow, making it
superb for in-track speed, but almost useless off
set tracks.

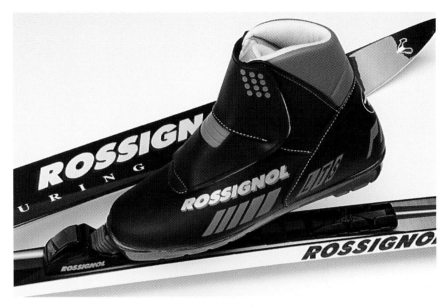

A typical sleek touring boot with NNN (New Nordic Norm) binding. Such boot/binding systems are ideal for skiing in set tracks or for day touring, but they are neither warm enough nor do they provide enough support for backcountry treks.

backcountry skis are akin to downhill models. They have metal edges that let you turn on hard snow and ice or steep terrain, they are wider than touring models, and they have the side cut and less pronounced camber typical of downhill models. With these skis you are able to go above the tree line, where the snow is scorched and windblown, and cut sharp turns on the way down. Those who like to kick around in the woods or on snow-covered roads will use a thinner touring ski without the metal edges. Backcountry skiers who like to cut Telemark and parallel turns often choose "fat boys," chunky, short, wide, metal-edged skis with a lot of side cut that can handle deep powder, crud, and corn snow the way

a pig handles mud. The width of fat boys — as great as 80 mm — allows for additional side cut that enhances their turning characteristics.

BOOTS AND BINDINGS

Besides keeping your toes toasty, a good boot/binding system should provide both support and flexibility. You don't want your feet to feel that they're chewing-gummed to the ski, yet you want a secure enough link between the two to allow you to make surefooted turns. The first order of business is to buy quality boots and make sure they fit properly. Don't skimp on boots; inexpensive ones tend to have flimsy, flexible soles without enough torsional rigidity to

keep your heel on the ski when you want to turn.

When you make a turn, you are pivoting on an axis somewhere between the toes and heel of your foot. Since the toes are locked in place, the heel absorbs the brunt of your intentions, and it will slide as far as the boot/binding allows it to go.

When you first try on a boot, do so with the same sock layering (see Chapter 8) that you would wear when skiing. Walk around first, making sure your feet don't slide around in the boot. Boots that are too tight, however, impede circulation and rob your feet of their defense against freezing.

Boot/Binding Systems

Boots and bindings come in several different styles. Traditional 75-mm designs (the point at which the toe is clasped into the binding plate is 75 mm wide, hence the numerical distinction) are compatible with any three-pin binding. The 75-mm boots and bindings are suited to general touring and backcountry touring. Most light touring, skating, and racing skis are fitted with one of several integrated boot/binding systems. These systems employ lighter and narrower boots and bindings that reduce friction in machine-set tracks. Their narrow profile is also advantageous to skaters when they are edging their skis.

Once you have found a comfortable boot to suit your snowbound pursuits, you'll need a binding system that matches. For classical touring, you want a binding that allows your heel to rise up and down, aiding your forward motion as you employ the diagonal stride. Skating bindings are stiffer, so that the heel doesn't stray as far from the boot and can get back to the business of edging more quickly. Backcountry bindings tend to be stiffer so that the heel can get back to turning more quickly and with greater support.

A good binding will strike the right balance between heel freedom of movement and heel/ankle support. If the foot is too busy twisting inside an ill-fitting boot, it cannot engage the ski to turn as precisely. Good bindings increase the likelihood that a boot will tell the ski to do what the skier wants.

Which Boots and Bindings Are Right for You?

TOURING. If you enjoy touring on set tracks but also like to break your own trails, you'll want low-cut 75-mm boots that fit as comfortably as a tennis sneaker, with good forward flex and sufficient heel support. The better the boot, the less you'll notice its presence once you're clipped in. When you're touring, you want to be able to move the heel up and down with little resistance, but you also want some lateral support. A three-pin binding locks the front of the sole down, so you lunge and bend from the ball of your foot.

Telemark/backcountry boot with 75 mm cable binding. These full-leather, insulated boots are made to provide plenty of warmth and support. A padded ankle collar helps keep snow out.

LIGHT TOURING. At touring centers the new binding systems have surpassed the trusty 75-mm three-pin arrangements, which may still suit your needs. The latest systems — the New Nordic Norm (NNN), Salomon Nordic Systems (SNS), and Skating Diagonal System (SDS) — integrate specific boot designs with compatible bindings.

The three systems incorporate a metal bar in the toe of your boot that locks into the binding system, creating a hinge between boot and ski. This lets you lift your heel farther from the ski — in fact, perpendicular to it — without the resistance found with 75-mm boot/bindings.

Since light tourers ski exclusively on machine-set tracks, their boots are low-cut with a narrow profile that will not create unwanted friction on the tracks. These bindings, however, provide neither enough support nor enough warmth, for off-track skiing.

SKATING. Because skaters push off the inside edges of their skis, causing their ankles to roll, skating boots are high-cut, have reinforced sides, and are very rigid at the heel. If you pronate (roll your heels inward while walking) or supinate (roll your heels outward), make sure your boot has a firm heel to absorb the brunt of burden on your insteps, ankles, and shins. Some people add platforms called footbeds to the inside of their boots to give the ankles additional support.

1) Skating (NNN system): A stiff, high-top model for racing and performance skating.
2) Combination (NNN system): A removable stiff cuff makes this model capable of double duty as a skating or a touring boot.
3) Touring (NNN system): Insulation and fleece lining give this boot the warmth needed for touring off set tracks.
4) Backcountry (75 mm): Insulated, full-leather model resembles a classic hiking boot. Note the groove around the heel, made to accept cable bindings.

BACKCOUNTRY.

Reminiscent of hiking boots, the footwear for off-trail skiing is heavier, warmer, and more durable than its touring cousins. Backcountry boots offer ample support to your feet and ankles when your body is encumbered by a backpack or when you make sharp downhill turns on nasty surfaces that can jolt the lower legs. But their design packs so much warmth and energy into the boot pocket, you'll need to be aware that blisters can develop very easily if you choose your socks carelessly or fail to break the boots in sufficiently. Be patient. Because these boots are made of full-grain leather, they require a long break-in period.

The standard 75-mm binding is the choice for the backcountry, often with the addition of removable heel clamps so that the boot can be held tightly to the ski when you're heading downhill, then freed to flex up and down when you're back on the flats and during climbs.

Many backcountry veterans and a few tourers still swear by the old-fashioned 75-mm cable bindings. With cable bindings, your foot is clamped down at the toe, while a steel cable wraps, harnesslike, around the heel of your boot. The cable provides a great deal of lateral stability for maneuvering on downhills and through powder, but restricts your ability to move your heel up and down.

POLES

Think of poles as extensions of your arms. Unlike alpine skiers, cross-country skiers need to use their arms and

Poles

1) Skating: The longest pole (up to the skier's chin), it should be stiff yet light.
2) Touring: An all-purpose pole, it should reach your armpit and be lightweight.
3) Telemark: A shorter pole with a larger basket for downhill powder.
4) Backcountry: Adjustable poles are great for treks where a long pole is best for touring, but a shorter pole is needed for long downhills.
5) Mountaineering: This pole converts into a 260-cm avalanche probe.

Baskets

1) Skating: Hardly a basket at all, it's designed to minimize wind resistance.
2) Touring: For skiing in set tracks or across a meadow.
3) Telemark: A larger basket prevents the pole from sinking into deep powder.
4) Mountaineering: This basket can be removed quickly, turning the pole into an avalanche probe.

upper body for forward locomotion —
and occasionally for braking. As you
become more practiced, you'll need
stiffer poles to handle the stress
required of them. If a pole bends too
much when you apply pressure to it,
then the pole is absorbing the
strength of your thrust and the
intended effect is diminished.

Pole length varies based not just
on use, but also on the height of the
skier. When you use a diagonal stride
on groomed tracks, your poles should
reach your armpit. Tourers on
untracked trails should look for poles
that reach their armpit or shoulder,
the additional length making up for
the poles' sinking down into
unpacked snow. If you switch to
skating, use poles that reach your
chin or nose, since you will swing
your arms in a greater arc. Skaters
also look for very tough, stiff poles
that can take the downward pressure
required as they initiate the skating
motion. If your skis have metal

The correct way to strap on a pair of cross-country ski poles.

edges, be sure to use aluminum
poles; the edges can chip bamboo or
fiberglass poles very easily.

Adjustable poles are especially
useful if you plan to ski in the backcountry. Extend them to help you
climb uphill and retract them before
you head down. Free-heeled skiers
who want to link Telemark and par-

GEAR TALK

BASKETS

The design of pole baskets seems as arbitrary as that of snowflake
shapes. They may seem to be fashion statements. In fact, basket shapes
vary with the snow they're for. Larger baskets keep poles from getting lost
in deep, soft snow; you can get that sinking feeling if your baskets don't
have the necessary surface area. Those who ski on groomed surfaces use
poles with smaller baskets that reduce weight and wind resistance.

Skaters use pole baskets that are shaped like trapezoids, with the
pole running through the short-end edge that sticks out from the pole.

GETTING A GRIP ON GRIPS

Cross-country poles are designed for left and right hands, and telling one from the other isn't always easy. The position of the grips and the straps — designed to fasten your poles around your wrists — indicate which pole fits which hand. Let the straps hang by the side of the pole and then slip your hand into the strap until it wraps around your palm. The top strap will lie over either the right or left side of the handle, corresponding to which hand belongs in each strap.

Come up through the loop and wrap your thumb and pointer finger around the handle, keeping the bottom strap below your palm at all times. Do not push your thumb down on the knob as though you were playing Space Invaders. As you extend your hands backward during the follow-through of the poling motion, your palms should let go of the pole so that only the thumb and pointer finger are touching it. Your backswing will be more fluid and natural if you let go of the pole. Gripping the pole too hard tends to stop your backswing prematurely. You have a better grip on skiing already.

allel turns appreciate the stability of a shorter pole and don't need the propulsion power of a longer one. Long poles will also further restrict you if you're wearing a backpack.

Although you probably won't need this feature, some poles convert to avalanche probes (see Chapter 9) that can better enable your group to locate you during a rescue effort.

WAXING

So what if you got an A in Dr. Poindexter's tenth-grade chemistry class? This is an entirely new application of molecular dynamics, foolproof as a weather forecast and clean as a cat's box. Still, this inexact science will help you ski better.

Why Wax?

Changeable temperatures and variable snow conditions and terrain dictate that some strides will be easier than others. And although you can bend your knees and turn your legs, you can't tell your skis when you need them to grip tightly or slide forgivingly — unless you wax them. Different waxes have various properties that allow you to kick (grip wax) and glide (glide wax).

Wax actually works by creating a temporary bond between itself and the snowflakes when a ski is pushed

down against the snow. As the ski glides, the friction causes the bond to break and the flakes to melt, leaving a thin sheet of water above the other layers of snow. Remember, it only takes a few drops of moisture to start you skidding about the shower tub. This water sheet creates a controlled skidding surface for your skis.

Almost 150 years ago, gold miners in the California hills raced against time, the elements, and other treasure hunters who had like visions of hidden nuggets. The most inventive miners began using animal skins to climb uphill, but for swifter descent they started greasing their ski bottoms with slick cocktails that made them slide faster. The potions included lard, castor oil, and pine pitch.

Waxless Skis

Of course, you can bag Chemistry 101 altogether by using waxless skis that have a pattern of steps or scales milled into the ski base. The patterns, like scales on a fish or the fur on a cat, are smooth when rubbed in one direction, but rough in the opposite direction. Just like a cat, a waxless ski base feels smooth when rubbed from tip to tail, but rough

Grip waxes (above) come in metal containers. The wax itself and the containers are color coded to correspond to a wide range of temperatures and snow conditions. Waxless skis employ fish scale patterns (below) that allow forward motion, but keep the ski from slipping backward.

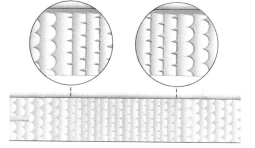

when rubbed from tail to tip. This allows the ski to glide forward, yet grip on the kick and when going uphill. Some argue that waxless skis work better than wax in changing snow conditions, in moist climates, or when the temperature hangs around 32°F. Those arguments stem in part from the fact that on warm days when the snow becomes wet, those with waxable skis must resort to messy, sticky klister waxes, the cross-

country equivalent of the tar baby. I know plenty of devotees of wax-able skis who keep a pair of wax-less skis on hand for such conditions. And plenty of skiers would rather avoid the bother of waxing altogether, klister or no klister.

Waxing is work. Some beginners will be intent on learning the basics and will limit themselves to friendly, groomed terrain, so they might not notice the difference in performance between a well-waxed ski and a basic waxless model. There is enough to remember, what with how to move, how to dress, how to get up after you fall, and so on, that you might want to use a waxless ski under all conditions for a while and give yourself one less thing to worry about.

Unfortunately, waxless skis show a dramatic drop-off in performance when snow conditions are at their best: fresh, cold powder. And while waxless skis may grip reasonably well on new powder or choppy ice, they are usually poor gliders. What's more, the materials can be brittle,

Once the grip wax is applied it must be smoothed out by rubbing it vigorously with a cork block (right). Should your choice of wax be incorrect or the conditions change, you must remove wax using sharp-edged scrapers (left).

causing the scales to wear out after prolonged use, leaving disposable — and replaceable — wax as a preferable option. Waxless skis are less common in dry climates, such as the rarefied air of the Colorado Rockies, where wax selection is simpler and conditions change less rapidly.

Temperature and Snow Conditions

All waxes are temperature-sensitive and interact differently with their underfooting. You can distinguish waxes both by their color and by the temperature range listed on the containers. Unfortunately, there isn't one standard rating system for wax, so you should be aware of the system that your particular brand employs.

In the most common system, a green wax is used for temperatures

between -5°F and 5°F, a blue wax for temperatures between 10°F and 25°F, and a purple wax for temperatures at or slightly above freezing. Red and yellow waxes are also available for days better spent at the beach. If conditions force you to split hairs, there is also a "special blue" wax that fits between the temperature ranges of green and blue, and an "extra blue" wax that fits between blue and purple for warmer days.

Likewise with green.

In a simplified two-wax system, a gold wax is used for dry snow and a silver wax for wet snow. If you can make a good snowball, use silver wax; if the snowball wimps out in your hands, use gold wax.

Other systems simply tell you to use this container when the temperature rises above freezing and that container when it drops below. Again, select one team of waxes that makes

GEAR TALK

CLIMBING SKINS

Climbing skins—originally fashioned of seal skins, now made of synthetics—allow you to ascend backcountry hills without wax by creating a surface area that is rough in one direction and smooth in the other direction. Especially on long, mountainous uphills and carrying the additional weight of a backpack, you need as much grip as possible, making skins invaluable.

continued on next page

CLIMBING SKINS
continued from previous page

Attachments range from buckles to straps to adhesives, but however you put them on, treat them with care. Skins bruise easily. You can leave them on during the descent, but the effect of wear is similar to burned tire rubber.

Skins attach better to ski bases when the skins are clean and the bases are warm. Be sure to let the skins dry off as soon as you bring them home or reach your backcountry hut. Bring along an extra bag to keep the skins clean during the trip. Be aware that even rugged skins are susceptible to tears caused by rocks; bring an extra pair on long backcountry trips.

PLASTIC SKINS Made of a durable stretch plastic, these skins are attached by a buckle and straps that go around the ski's center. They are easy to attach and remove and are great for really steep hills. Unfortunately, if you plan to ski downhill, you will have to remove them, since they will stick and not allow you to slide down.

PLUSH-PILE SKINS Made of either super-slick mohair or a rugged nylon-derivative or both, these skins attach to the ski with a metal D-ring around the tip and a glue like adhesive that must be applied indoors and is prone to pick up dirt and gook. When you take them off in the backcountry, you must be extremely careful to stick them back-to-back so they don't attract gook. However, because the adhesive leaves the edges exposed, it allows skiers an easier time of it when edging their way uphill (see Chapter 4 for uphill techniques).

The plush-pile climbing skins can also be attached with a hook-and-buckle arrangement that is very effective at keeping the skin on the skis. The hooked tip and buckled tail are supported by a Velcro strap along the middle. This arrangement is the least messy of the three, though the grip may be stronger when you use the other two. If you're climbing a moderate hill, this is a good option.

you comfortable and ask local residents which snow conditions and waxes are most common in the area.

As a rule, the warmer the weather, the softer the wax. Use a wax that is too hard, and "Get a grip" will have new meaning as

Snow conditions can change while you're skiing, so always carry extra waxes. If snow begins to stick to your skis, don't suffer. Stop, clean the snow off, and try another wax.

you slide backward down the uphill. Use a wax that is too soft, and ice may start to form on the bottom of your skis after the wax has picked up too much snow.

Keep in mind that fresh-fallen snow is flaky and crumbles in your hand; older, warmer, wetter snow packs into a snowball. Temperatures close to freezing are the most troublesome, since water alters its composition at the freezing point. If caught at 32 degrees, find a coin for flipping or carry a tiny thermometer that attaches to a zipper tab and can give you an instant reading. Or resort to that pair of waxless skis.

Kick Zone vs. Glide Zone
They sound like football formations, but they're sections of your ski that

may require different types of wax. Remember, when you push off or transfer your body's weight, you're placing downward pressure on the midsection, or camber, of the ski, so that it will grip the snow. The ski belly is known as the kick zone or wax pocket. As you glide on one or both skis, you're releasing the pressure (unweighting), leaving only the tip and tail to glide along the snow. The ski's ends form the glide zone. Apply grip wax only in the kick zone, a 2½-foot midsection of the ski beneath and just forward of your ski boot.

Types of Waxes
Since different parts of your skis have different functions, an arrangement of waxes is set up to facilitate

their tasks. Skiers generally use two types: a sticky "grip wax" that improves uphill traction and prevents you from sliding backward, and a "glide wax" that is slithery and creates a more slippery interaction between ski and snow, allowing you to glide faster and more smoothly on flat surfaces and downhills. When navigating older, warmer, tattered snow, you may need to use klister, the useful but user-unfriendly gook that guides the kick zone through spring slop and makes you appreciate the cold days when you don't have to use it.

Grip Wax Application

Before applying any wax, clean the ski of snow and debris by running your gloved hand all the way down the underside. Then apply the firm wax onto the ski base as though you were writing your name on the ski with a crayon. Start rubbing about 6 inches above the heel plate and stop rubbing about 15 to 18 inches below the tip. Remember, only the camber pocket needs grip wax. In all you will probably need to wax about 2½ feet of the ski base.

After applying a thin, uniform layer of grip wax, use a block of cork to smooth the wax onto the ski surface, firmly rubbing down the ski. Allow the wax to cool and reach air temperature, since you apply it at room temperature. Then test the hold of your grip wax by skiing for a few minutes, finding a small uphill as a gauge. You'll need to ski for more than a few strides to make sure you've got it right. If you're still slipping, create a longer kick zone by adding a wax layer farther toward the ski's tip. If that doesn't work, try applying the next-softer wax you have available.

If you need to err on one side or other, start with a hard (colder) wax. If the wax is too hard, simply place the softer (warmer) wax on top of it. You cannot put a hard wax on a soft wax, but you can put a soft wax on a hard wax. If your wax is too soft, you'll need to scrape it off before you can apply a harder version. At some point you just have to ski. Use more forceful strides to help you get more out of the wax. If your wax seems fine for a while, but seems less effective later, the wax has probably started to wear off. Don't be concerned and don't suffer with backsliding. Simply stop and reapply.

Klister

A gooey cross between maple syrup and rubber cement, klister is an adherent you apply to your skis as you would a dab of toothpaste. Use a scraper to spread it down the length of the ski, making sure not to spread any in the groove down the middle of the ski. Beware: Klister is the messiest word in skiing, and if you let it touch your hands, it will touch everything that touches your hands. And stay there. For many skiers, klister is either a last resort or a non-

resort; they'd rather skip skiing altogether and wait for the temperature to drop.

Trouble is, klister is the best defense against crabby, wet, elderly snow, which is often found around machine-set tracks. Suppose over the course of a week the snow has melted on Monday, frozen on Tuesday, and crackled on Wednesday. Follow that with a Thursday sprinkling, a Friday hail pelting, and a Saturday windstorm, and the snow starts to wrinkle with age.

Klister bonds better to fractured granules and fragments than regular grip wax. It has a high freezing point and needs warmth for proper application, which should be done indoors, if possible, using a plastic spreader. Some skiers who don't care to search for warm places bring a torch or iron to heat the gook, thereby bonding it more tightly to the ski for a surer hold. Be sure to stash the klister in a warm place, and be equally sure to tighten the top securely and keep the container away from sharp objects that can puncture the outside and spill the klister.

Glide Wax Application

Cloaking your skis in glide wax is time-consuming, and many skiers ignore the glide zone entirely. Unlike grip wax, which can easily be applied outdoors, glide wax prefers the warm, dry air of your living room. It is common practice to coat the ski with glide wax once in a while and then apply grip wax over it for each ski outing, though this often interferes with the grip wax's adhesion to the ski. As a rule, skaters wax the entire ski with glide wax for extra slide. Classical skiers either use glide wax in the glide zone only or they rely on the base itself and use none at all.

Before waxing, rub some sandpaper along the base to remove debris and residue of old wax. Then heat the glide wax to make it drip onto the ski. You may want to use a simple hand-held lighter or even matches to melt the wax, but you'll need a heated iron to spread the melted wax along the ski base. Make

A torch makes evenly spreading klister outdoors an easy task. It can also be used to soften old wax before removing it.

from stoves and fireplaces, since you're dealing with a flammable substance. Allow the solvent to loosen the wax for a few minutes. Then wipe off the ski with a cloth.

Heating the ski briefly with a torch — don't do this if you've already used wax remover — will also loosen the wax and allow you to clean with a warm cloth.

CARE AND STORAGE

It's springtime. You've dusted off the tennis racket, the rod, and the pitching wedge, but what are you going to do with your skis? And those boots — the last time you left them and forgot about them, you had a hard time believing that the odd origami crumple used to house your feet.

Off-season storage is not difficult. Your collective sweat for boot, binding, and pole maintenance should take about 20 minutes. Ski preservation is more time-consuming, but less expensive than buying a new pair each time the leaves fall.

BOOTS AND BINDINGS. In a 1953 column, renowned columnist and not so renowned ski expert Art Buchwald once answered a woman's letter with the following advice: "Wearing ski boots in the snow is the worst thing that you can do with them. Good ski boots are hard to come by and should only be used for dancing and bowling. If your husband insists on taking walks, make him buy you a

sure to use a low setting so that the wax drips slowly and evenly, but doesn't burn the ski or set off a smoke detector. Wait for the wax to set and then scrape off the excess with a plastic scraper knife.

Removing Wax

Après-ski care is akin to cleaning dishes after dinner — but it has to be done. First, scrape off what you can with a metal scraper made to clean skis. Before you apply a liquid solvent onto the base, make sure to put on a good pair of plastic or rubber gloves, since many of these solvents are toxic. If you can't find a nontoxic wax remover, be sure to stay away

pair of galoshes."

We've all come in from the rain and left a pair of leather shoes to dry hoping they wouldn't lose their shape. The next morning, the sensation of screwing them back on is like choking your feet.

Fortunately, even the most flimsy ski boot is made of fibers more resistant to weather's whim. But any practice you've had in caring for those leather shoes will come in handy as your boots head for hibernation.

After each use, let boots dry out slowly. Keep them in dry but cool surroundings and let them air out. This will preserve the fibers while discouraging mold, mildew, and fungus. Never speed the process by putting boots near a woodstove, fireplace, or radiator; this quickly damages the leather. Remember, the air in your house is extremely dry all winter, so your boots will dry without added encouragement. If mildew appears, wet the spot and wash with bleach. Treat boots regularly with protective wax such as Biwell, Snoseal, or Nikwax (basing your choice on the boot manufacturer's recommendation) to prevent the leather from drying out and shrinking and cracking. Before storing your boots for the summer, make sure they are completely dry and apply another coat of conditioner. If your boots have removable liners, remove them and stuff the insides with paper towels.

Be sure to scrub dirt and grime from the bindings in order to protect them; a dirt clump, a pebble, or salt can cause bindings to rust over the summer. Before storing them, spray a nonabrasive silicone onto the binding area of both the ski and the boot toe if the binding system includes metal hinge bars.

SKIS. Like boots, skis should be dry before you tinker with them. Assuming there are no noticeable cracks that need to be filled with P-Tex wax, it's time to work on the ski bases. First, thoroughly rub down the base with a wax-removing solvent. Rub the base shortly after with a nonabrasive pad.

It's a good idea to apply a protective base wax, making certain to cover the steel edges of backcountry skis to protect them against oxidation. An off-season ski tune at a local ski shop is advisable, and will save you the bother of filling cracks or gouges. The shop will apply a light, protective base wax that will not interfere with other waxes you may use.

When storing skis, stand them up as you see them standing in a ski shop: tails down, tips up, base toward the wall. When standing, today's skis shouldn't lose their camber. Keep them away from concrete floors, whose chemicals can react with the skis' aluminum compounds, causing damage.

POLES. Ah, the easy part. Remember the old VW rabbit that ran on and on no matter what you did to it? The cars have been condensed into ski

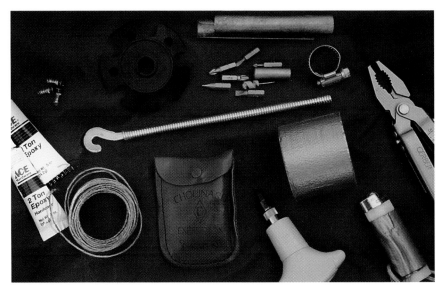

Ski Repair Kit. Clockwise from top: spare ski pole basket; channel metal and hose clamp for pole repair; Gerber multitool pliers (with various bits, left of hose clamp); lighter; duct tape; ratcheted screwdriver; emergency sewing kit; wire; spare binding cable (long rod at center); epoxy; spare binding screws. Your own kit, of course, must be customized to your gear.

poles. Give the poles one quick soap-and-water cleaning. Other than that, remember where you put them. And store them where kids can't find them; they make superb spears in the wrong hands.

GEAR TALK

SKI REPAIR

Wax can even plug deep scrapes and gashes in your ski base. Keep some of your hard base wax handy in case you happen to glide across saber-tooth ice and rock fragments, traverse a bed of thumb tacks or drop your ski on a porcupine. The base wax will temporarily fill the holes and allow you to finish the day's tour.

You still need to use a molten plastic (P-Tex) candle in order to fill the crevasses for good. Clean excess wax from the affected area and drip the melted wax of a P-Tex candle onto the wounds. Hold the candle away from your hand and above the ski, so neither gets scorched. Allow the ski to cool until the P-Tex hardens, and then scrape away the overflow.

O N
T H E
L E V E L

You've seen pitchers tossing lightly in the bullpen before taking the mound. You've seen runners lifting a leg onto a park bench and reaching across their bodies to touch their toes before an early-morning jog. The trouble is that not enough cross-country skiers bother to stretch before hitting the trails. There is so much anticipation and so much to think about: *Is my gear right? What's the wind like? What's the snow like? Do I have the right wax? How fast can I get out there? Are there many people out today?* The idea of elongating the muscles is a stretch for most people, who just want to get out and ski while the snow conditions are good. But ironically, the incidence of injury is so infrequent in cross-country skiing, it's likely that more injuries are caused by improper preparation off the trails than by improper execution on them.

Cross-country skiers have even more reason to stretch than runners do. Most runners spend a few minutes walking to their start line, whether it's a park entrance, a roadway, or a school track. That walk begins flexing the muscles. But most skiers cramp their legs into a car and have barely stepped onto the snow by the time they put on their skis. Also keep in mind that cold weather tightens muscles.

The trusty diagonal stride, foundation of cross-country skiing, will see you around the set tracks of a Nordic center and through uncharted terrain like this.

Nordic skiing can be a simple form of relaxing exercise. But if you're not used to some sort of regular exertion, give yourself some time to build a fitness base from which to work. This need not apply to people who are generally active, and it need not entail more than a few long walks, scenic bike rides, or tennis matches for those who aren't. Even swimming a few laps at the local Y can prepare you. If you have the urge to experiment with cross-country skiing or to make it the centerpiece

TECHNIQUE TIP

ON TRACK

You may be tentative about stepping into machine set tracks for the first time, but they are a great help. The tracks control the direction of the skis and prevent them from slipping left or right — kind of like bicycle training wheels. The grooves will keep your tips from crossing, though you should still be aware of keeping your weight slightly forward and centered over your skis. Don't become dependent on set tracks; you want to get a feel for as many different snow conditions as possible from the outset.

of your cardiovascular itinerary, take
a few days or weeks, depending on
your state of decay, to acclimate your
body to the fun it's going to have.
(For a more thorough pre-ski stretch,
see "Loosening Up to Ski," page 59.)

READY, SET. . .
Taking Lessons

When you aren't linking stylish
turns, you still need to link skills,
even for the most basic forms of
skiing. Taking certified instruction
at a Nordic center will help reassure
you that your form is polished enough
to turn the next page. You may sail
through the introductory steps of the

Falling down is as easy as it looks — and can be
the best way to stop. Getting up is far easier
than most people make it look.

diagonal stride, but if you start
stalling on the uphills, an instructor
can give you some optional drills you
might never have tried on your own.

FALLING AND
GETTING UP

Moving along reasonably smoothly,
you glance to your left and catch a
glimpse of another skier. Trouble
is, your distracted ski has caught
only a glimpse of the set tracks.
You lean back to get a closer look
and suddenly you're swimming
like a fish. Forget it. Once you're
far past the vertical, you're also
past the point of no return. But
instead of cushioning your collapse, you try to save face. Shake
a leg, you figure. Parry the air with
your poles. Something, anything,
so it doesn't look like an f-a-l-l.

Know what? Bag the tributes
to style points. They prolong the
fall, annoy the skier, and leave
you with pretzel empathy. Swing
your arms like a propeller all you
want; you're still going to fall. Predictable and unavoidable, falls
seem to take place in slow motion,
yet they still rattle you enough to
leave you with doubts about your
equilibrium. They are skiing's
answer to sneezes. Your attention
to subtle correction produces the
gradual compounding of flaw upon
glitch until. . . *ohmygoshnever-
mind*. . . . womp!

The tattering tease of *womp*
can be as humiliating as a mid-

continued on next page

recital hiccup. But don't worry about a fall. It's the world's favorite stopping technique. The important surfaces — yours and the snow's — are well padded. What's more, there are ways to fall safely.

When you feel a fall coming on, lower yourself so you're closer to the ground. Bring your hands closer to your body so you don't jam a finger against your ski or strain a shoulder. If when you finally come to a full stop you have legs wrapped around arms wrapped around skis stuck to poles, try rolling onto your back and shaking things out in the air. Then roll over onto your hands and knees (1), making sure your skis are across the slope (assuming you didn't fall at the bottom of the hill) and flat on the snow with your knees on top of the skis (2). Slide one ski forward and pick yourself up (3). Dusting is optional (4). Quitting is forbidden.

Ask around to find an instructor with a good reputation. Who is helpful? Patient? Experienced? For the beginner, a Nordic center with superior facilities is not as useful as a modest place with an inspired teacher. Group instruction with skiers of varied abilities is usually a bad idea for a beginner. Such lessons inevitably proceed too quickly for you at times and too slowly at other times.

Baby Steps

Clipped into your skis, carbo-loaded, stretched, and properly attired, you're ready to go. So just how do you go? Skis don't come with ignition keys, and they sure make you feel awkward. You look at the snow. You look at your skis. You adjust your well-adjusted poles, looking for answers they don't have. Nothing. So you try

Double-poling is a good way to get around on flats or gentle downhills. This skier demonstrates near perfect form on the follow-through.

striding. Mistake. The wrong things moved in the wrong directions. Now you have a close-up view of the day's snow conditions.

If you've never been on skis before, forget about skiing for a few moments. Take some time to get used to your big slippers by walking on them. If you need to take exaggerated steps to move your feet forward, so be it. Choose a flat piece of land and go for a stroll, picking your skis right off

the snow as you would your feet off the ground. Then begin leaning forward and tilting left and right and start bending your knees a bit as you take each step. Don't worry about concepts such as "weight transfer" yet. Just get comfortable leaning over each ski.

As you walk on the skis, concentrate on keeping their tips from crossing. Guide them straight and parallel. If you've ever been in a sack

Diagonal Stride

1) KICK: Push straight down through your boot and the midsection of your ski as you initiate the *kick* with your left leg. Your knees and ankles should be slightly flexed and your torso leaning forward.

2) GLIDE & POLE PUSH: Now your weight has shifted to your right leg, which is driven forward and down the track in the *glide*. Your opposite arm naturally follows suit, coming forward for the *pole plant*. The elbow of this forward arm should be slightly bent for maximum power in the *pole push*.

3) KICK: The push is timed just before the initiation of a kick with your right leg.

4) GLIDE & POLE PUSH: Now weight shifts to your left, or gliding leg, and the sequence begins all over again 5) & 6).

race when you couldn't move each leg separately, you'll appreciate the importance of not allowing one ski tip to step on the other. Also, get used to the idea that your footwear has very little traction. Think of walking on a slippery floor with shoes. It's hard to describe just how your gait employs scoot-prevention, but if somebody tells you to watch out for the wet floor, you're just as likely to skid, but somehow less likely to fall because you're bracing for the sudden slide.

DIAGONAL STRIDE

This stride is so-called not because you'll be traveling sideways like a bishop in a chess game, but because of the line created when the right arm swings back as the left leg moves forward and the left arm swings forward as the right leg pushes off. The diagonal stride is the most common step in cross-country skiing. Think of the

sequence as one kick-and-glide after another, a motion that approximates walking with exaggerated yet very graceful motion.

Start to Kick

Shift your weight onto one ski again as you did when you first stepped onto the snow and began to get the feel of the skis. With your feet still parallel, bend your knees and begin pushing down — not back — with one foot on one ski. Keep your hips over the ski that is pushing off. Keep your chest and hips forward and don't be fooled by the illusion that diagonal striders are kicking backward. Keep your weight on your whole foot as you push down.

As you pull the leg that has just pushed off forward so it is again even

T E C H N I Q U E   T I P

SKIING WITHOUT POLES

Most of us instinctively grip the poles too tightly, pushing them as though they were ejector buttons in a James Bond movie or pulling them like sticky levers in a Las Vegas slot machine. Poles can be very useful daggers when you start double-poling or climbing uphill, but they are intended for balance as well as propulsion.

The best way to learn proper balance that will enable you to maximize pole usage is to try skiing without them. Leave the poles behind and let the arms swing normally, in sync with the legs. Swing the right arm forward with the left leg and the left arm forward with the right leg, and be sure to swing the arms in front of your body rather than across it. Begin springing forward off each leg, driving forward with the hips. The more comfortable you get, the more glide you'll produce, and the more weight you'll start putting on the kicking ski as you drive the wax pocket of the ski down, and then onto the glide ski immediately thereafter in preparation for it to bear down into the next kick.

with the gliding leg, begin to shift your weight to the gliding ski in preparation to put your full weight on it as you kick off.

Start to Glide

When gliding, always bend slightly at the knees, but don't hunch the upper body. Keep your hips forward with your hands in front of you, and keep all your weight on the gliding leg. Also be sure to bend your ankles and keep your entire leg flex-ible. Straighten and stiffen your gliding leg only after it passes under you and gets ready to kick.

Diagonal stride: This skier has just kicked with her right ski and is gliding on her left ski. Once mastered, the diagonal stride will propel you almost effortlessly down miles of track.

Using the Poles

Think of walking at a fast pace. How do you swing your arms? As you slide forward on your right ski, your opposite arm will naturally swing for-ward with it. You could almost be in marching formation the way your steps follow one another. Hup-two. Hup-two.

To do this with poles, bring your arm near chest level, keeping your elbow slightly bent as you go. Swing back down with the arm, propelling

off the snow and allowing it to follow through behind your back in concert with the opposite leg. Make sure to keep your poles close to your sides as you plant them in the snow and push off; if you plant them too far out to the sides, you're not going to propel yourself forward as effectively.

Remember to release the pole at the end of each backswing. Extend your arm so the pole is close to vertical, but still angled backward. If you go past vertical and your weight pushes the poles so they extend far in front of you, prepare to sprawl.

The Star Turn

Beginners will like the star turn because it takes place on a flat surface and begins with the skier in a stationary position. The turn creates a pointy design with as many points as the steps you take, hence the name. With your ski tails together, lift one ski tip in the direction you're turning. First, place that ski on the snow, and then bring the other ski around next to it. Leaving your ski tails on the snow, keep placing your legs closer to the direction you want until you get there. Then ski on. The step turn (see Chapter 5) combines the star turn with forward momentum.

DOUBLE-POLING

Straight downhills with small drops and lengthy runouts give your legs a chance to take a breather by leaving it up to your arms and shoulders to hoist you along. If the track is especially fast or choppy, double-poling is also a secure means of maintaining your balance. Your weight is centered in between your legs, which act as anchors, since they remain even with each other during the poling action and don't extend as they do during the diagonal stride. Keep the poles under your shoulders and don't let them splay out to the sides, which detracts from the power of the poling motion.

PRE-POLING. Start by leaning slightly forward as you would in order to plant a single pole in the diagonal stride. Bring your hands to shoulder level and keep your hips directly

TECHNIQUE TIP

NAIL DOWN THOSE KICKS

Deb Ackerman, chairman of the Professional Ski Instructors of America's Nordic Education Committee, offers this device for thinking about kicking into glides: "When you start to kick off, pretend you have nails attached to the bottom of your feet (heel to toe) that go through your skis into the snow. Engage every nail as you kick off."

The kick double-pole is a great way to maintain speed when you hit a patch of slower snow or are striding across a meadow into a head wind.

TECHNIQUE TIP

SING WHILE YOU SWING

Sometimes novice skiers waste energy by trying consciously to move the right arm and the left leg in sync. The stride should come naturally. "When trying to remember which arm goes with which ski, you'll almost always get it wrong. So feel relaxed and try to think of a favorite song to establish rhythm and flow," advises Paul Peterson, coach of the Professional Ski Instructors of America Nordic Team.

over your toes.

To get even more thrust, lean farther forward and plant your poles farther in front of you to coil them backward with greater force. A word of caution: don't plant your poles so far ahead that they slide forward in front of you. If you don't pull the poles back, you will swan-dive, arms extended, into whatever is in front of you — quite possibly your ski tips.

Make sure your elbows are slightly bent and your poles are planted near your skis at a backward angle. As you become more proficient at double-poling, you'll extend the stroke by elongating your arms and bringing your poles close to, but short of, the vertical position.

POLING. Push down using the collective oomph of your upper body, including arms, shoulders, and upper back. You'll need all three in order to follow through properly. Be sure to take your arms behind you — to hip height, if possible — and release your grip on the poles at the end of the backswing. Remember, you want your arms to go back on the follow-through. Don't cheat by tilting your poles up unless you want to wave good-bye to the person behind you and so long to your hope of learning a good double-pole. Your hips should stay over your feet, but at the peak of the lean — as your poles are about to come off the snow — your back should be almost parallel to the ground. Your back should start to straighten shortly before your arms

66 There is nothing peculiarly malignant in the appearance of a pair of skis. They are two slips of elm wood, 8 feet long, 4 inches broad, with a square heel, turned-up toes, and straps in the center to secure your feet. No one, to look at them, would guess at the possibilities which lurk in them. But you put them on, and you turn with a smile to see whether your friends are looking at you, and then the next moment you are boring your head madly into a snowbank and kicking frantically with both feet, and half-rising, only to butt viciously into that snowbank again, and your friends are getting more entertainment than they had ever thought you capable of giving. 99

—Sir Arthur Conan Doyle

and poles reach a parallel position behind your back.

POST-POLING. After each push, return to a near-upright position quickly. Don't bend your knees as low and don't lean as far forward as you would in a tucked position, or you'll shorten the start point for the double-

continued on page 60

The Kick Double-Pole

1) **KICK:** Kick as you bring both poles forward in preparation for the pole plant.
2) **POLE PLANT:** You are poised to push off powerfully with both poles.
3) **DRIVE THE POLES:** With weight centered over both skis, compress your torso to drive both poles down and back.
4) **FOLLOW-THROUGH:** Let arms swing back freely as you complete the glide and prepare for the next kick as the poles come forward together.

▪

TECHNIQUE TIP

HEADS UP

When they should focus on the terrain straight ahead of them, novice skiers instead want to look at their footwork and at the ground immediately beneath them to make sure everything is OK. To counteract this understandable urge, Paul Peterson, coach of the Professional Ski Instructors of America Nordic Team and director of skiing at Bear Valley (California) Cross Country, suggests keeping this mantra in mind: "It is OK to look at your feet, but it is not polite to stare."

LOOSENING UP TO SKI

Everybody should stretch. To wash off some of the cobwebs and reduce the risk of afterburn, consider a few simple stretches and swivels. Even a few minutes of stretching before you hit the trail will make a big difference. For a 12-minute set of 21 stretches for cross-country skiers — and a definitive guide to stretching for all sports and activities — see *Stretching*, by Bob Anderson, from which the following stretches are adapted.

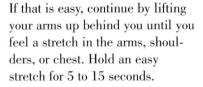

BACK, SHOULDERS, AND ARMS

From a standing position, with your knees slightly bent, gently pull your elbow behind your head as you bend from the hips to one side. Hold the stretch for 10 seconds. Repeat on other side.

SHOULDERS AND ARMS

Interlace your fingers behind your back. Now slowly turn your elbows inward while your straighten your arms.

If that is easy, continue by lifting your arms up behind you until you feel a stretch in the arms, shoulders, or chest. Hold an easy stretch for 5 to 15 seconds.

CALF AND ACHILLES TENDON

Bracing yourself against a wall with one hand over the other and your feet about 2 feet from the wall, bring your right leg forward and bend it at the knee. Moving your torso toward the wall, gently extend the calf and Achilles tendon of your left leg, keeping your left foot flat on the floor. Now change to the other leg.

HAMSTRINGS AND LOWER BACK

Sitting on the ground or floor, tuck your right foot into your groin. Straighten your left leg and reach as far forward as you comfortably can. Hold that position for 30 seconds, then change to the other leg.

continued from page 57

poling motion, thereby minimizing
the impact — and distance — of
each thrust.

The Kick Double-Pole

Okay, try dipping your kick-and-
glide into your double-pole and
seeing what the recipe yields. The
dish you take out of the oven is
another way to maintain speed that
will allow you to go even faster, but
won't permit quite the same respite
for your legs. The technique is especially useful if the track slows down
or a headwind kicks up.

As you start to swing both poles
forward, begin to kick one leg,
pushing down the way you would
with the follow-through of a pole
push. Leave the other foot in the
track so it becomes your gliding leg.
Plant your poles shortly before your
trail leg has caught up to your gliding
leg, so as not to inhibit the length of
the glide. If the kicking leg tires, try
switching legs to give it a rest. Getting everything in sync may take a
while, and at least at the start you
may prefer to establish a more robust
double-pole rather than tangle with
too many moving limbs at once.

GOING
UPHILL

As in any cross-country sport — whether running, bicycling, or skiing — how you ascend a hill depends on how steep the hill is and how much stamina you have. Those in top condition sprint the entire way up; others set a slow, steady pace; still others wind up walking the steepest pitch. No matter, just so you reach the top.

With cross-country skiing, going uphill also depends on variable snow conditions and your ability to match those conditions with the right wax. Those considerations, as well as your physical condition, can dictate which of the following approaches you take. But if you remember only one thing

on ascents, let it be this: slow and steady will always serve you well. Don't even think about trying to maintain speed, just maintain a steady forward pace. Like the experienced bicyclist who shifts into very low gears to save his legs even as he spins the pedals faster and gives up speed, think about taking many more and shorter strides, slowing your pace, and expending your energy carefully. Forget about trying to sprint to the top; you'll only arrive there in a heart-pounding sweat.

Think of the following techniques as progressing from a relatively high gear to the lowest gear. A higher gear may be all you need for a

Diagonal Stride Uphill

1) Press your kicking ski (right leg) firmly downward so your wax (or waxless pattern) can grip the snow more effciently. Meanwhile, move your opposite leg forward.
2) Reach up the hill, making a solid pole plant as you shift your weight to your left ski.
3) Keep your weight directly over your skis as you press down on your left ski to kick again. If your weight shifts too far forward, your skis will slide back downhill.
4) Reach up the hill for the next pole plant, again keeping your weight over the skis.

slight, short uphill. For a longer rise that becomes steeper, you'll need to employ all the gears, starting with the highest and shifting down.

One last tip: don't look down at your ski tips or the track just ahead of you when skiing uphill. Hold your head up and look at the trail well ahead of you. That way you can anticipate increases or decreases in slope. And keeping your head held high helps prevent your torso from slouching into the bent-over position that puts too much of your weight on the ski forward of the wax pocket, where it does you no good. You want your weight over your boots.

Diagonal Stride Uphill

To return to the cycling analogy, the diagonal stride uphill is similar to taking on a small hill without down-

shifting, but instead anticipating the hill, gaining some extra momentum before you hit it, and putting in some extra effort — maybe even standing on the pedals — as you ascend. It's a very satisfying feeling, because you never miss a beat by having to shift gears, but rather take the hill and head over the top exhilarated and ready to take on the next hill with greater confidence.

The two key points to remember are that your diagonal stride uphill becomes mostly kick and very little glide and that you'll be relying on your upper body and poles for more of your forward momentum than on the flats.

So, before you reach the base of the hill, gain a little extra speed. Then be prepared to shorten your stride considerably and almost jog

uphill. It's critical when ascending to push down on the snow so that your wax (or waxless pattern) grips the snow as efficiently as possible. At the same time, you must keep your knees bent and your body leaning slightly forward over your gliding ski. But don't lean too far forward, or your skis will tend to slip downhill, landing you on your face.

It may seem contradictory, but you must maintain a light step on uphill strides while at the same time pushing down aggressively on the kick so the wax can do its job. The light step keeps you from slipping backward and anticipates the fact that with every small stride forward, you are also taking a step up. Again, it might help to think about bicycling: you've stayed in a high gear, are approaching the crest, and must stand up on your pedals to keep going. You're applying plenty of force on the pedals, but you're doing so with your body forward and with a

---

TECHNIQUE TIP

PULL OVER!

On machined-groomed, heavily used trails, the snow becomes packed, especially in the middle of the trail. That packed snow is an ally on the flats and going downhill, because it enhances your glide. On inclines, however, it's your enemy, because it makes it more difficult for your wax (or waxless pattern) to grip.

The solution? Pull over to the side of the trail where the snow is softer, deeper, less worn, and more grip-friendly. In this case, the right lane is the passing lane. Just see that you don't catch a tip on the underbrush in the process.

The herringbone is a decided downshift to climb hills too steep to stride or walk up.

light, energized touch.

Don't forget to let your pace slow, and shorten your steps. You should also think about keeping the wax pocket on the snow almost continuously, so that you proceed in a sort of light-footed shuffle with your weight coming down over the midsection of your skis.

The Herringbone

Charlie Chaplin goes skiing. Starring you — and everyone else employing this very useful means of traipsing uphill, so don't be shy about it. Among other things, your herringbone technique will be helpful in learning how to skate, since the steps are similar to the V-1 skating technique explained in Chapter 6. Bushy eyebrows are optional, though twirling your pole is not advised.

The herringbone is a decided downshift. Make sure to go into it just before you really need to so that you won't stall out. First spread your skis into a V, splitting the tips wide apart and making sure not to cross the tails. Bend your knees slightly toward each other, forcing your skis to lean to their inner edges. Now dig in and prepare to walk purposefully — but again lightly — on your skis. You'll need to push off with your edges and plant your poles into the snow so you don't slide back. Remember to push off down and behind you with the poles, centering your weight on each ski as you step. Move the right arm and left leg simultaneously. Then do the same with the left arm and right leg. Use your arms liberally and remain upright, head high, looking far forward. Hunching makes the lungs smaller. Be sure to move the legs directly uphill, and don't take hesitant steps. Slide them too far to the side, and you'll wish you had paid attention on gymnastics day in your fourth-grade P.E. class.

The Running Herringbone

Sounds like one of Woody Hayes's more bizarre gadget plays, performed

A more advanced step, the running herringbone is akin to skating uphill and allows you to maintain greater speed. It also requires more conditioning.

your skis' wax-less pattern — isn't gripping as it should. This is another downshift; you're taking even more steps for the amount of ground covered, but you're conserving energy in the process, ensuring that you'll crest the hill.

Besides picking up your legs in more rapid succession, make sure to use your poles fre-

With the herringbone, it is important to shift your weight completely from side to side and keep your head up, eyes focused out in front.

out of the wishbone formation. Either that or spoiled fish. In fact, it is a good way to enhance the effect of the herringbone when the slope is especially steep or your grip wax — or quently, and don't go so fast that you compromise the angle of the edge, which must still lean toward the uphill so the ski can push off against the snow.

TECHNIQUE TIP

HERRINGBONE QUACK

"With the herringbone, it is important to shift your weight completely from side to side," says Paul Peterson, coach of the Professional Ski Instructors of America Nordic Team. "Think of waddling like a duck. To make yourself waddle, try quacking out loud as you move up the hill."

The Sidestep

The sidestep is as graceful as the funky-chicken tango, only much slower. Still, the sidestep is the most secure means of avoiding bad footing — in your case, that one step that will shoot you spiraling downward. Use it on really steep hills or icy drifts, places where the conditions may make the swifter, but less sure-footed, herringbone an imprudent option. You are now in low-low gear. There is nowhere else to shift.

Start by standing perpendicular to the hill, edging your ski uphill. Lift up from the knees rather than using the whole body. When the terrain gets steeper, you want the knees and ankles rolled uphill to get a nice edging. The upper body should be erect, not hunched. Angle your hips toward the uphill for more edge. If the hill is on your right side, lift the right foot up the hill followed by the left foot up to within 2 or 3 inches of the right foot, as if you were climbing stairs sideways. Don't try to take large steps. Remember to keep your head up and dig your ski poles into the snow while keeping them outside the skis. Dig your ski edges into the snow directly across the slope of the

IT CAN HAPPEN TO ANYONE

In case you think accidents only happen to you, consider what happened in March 1994 to Olympic hopeful Lara Bergel at the U.S. Junior National Championships in Bend, Oregon. Bergel, a Dartmouth College sophomore, was leading the 10-kilometer classical final with 2 kilometers to go when she reached a short, sharp uphill slope. Because of the race's staggered start, Bergel was skiing unaccompanied. She received word from her coaches that she was posting the day's fastest intermediate split times.

Bergel had been double-poling and had begun using a running herringbone to ascend the mound, her last serious obstacle to victory, when mortality struck. "I got three-quarters of the way up the hill, stuck my pole in between my skis, and started sliding all the way back down," Bergel recalls. "Junior Nationals, and there I am sliding on my stomach. I couldn't believe I did that."

Bergel skidded to a stop, regrouped, stumbled again, and began herringboning furiously to atone for lost time. Her spill added half a minute to an otherwise stellar time that left her in third place — 30 seconds behind the champion.

Racers often double pole to maintain speed over gentle hills. These two racers demonstrate the high and low positions of the pole stroke.

tips up. Again, stay perpendicular to the slope. Given patience and a trail wide enough to accommodate the length of your skis, the sidestep will get you up the steepest of slopes. On a narrow trail, swallow your pride, take your skis off, and walk. It's a far nobler option than sliding backward over the steep ground you just climbed.

The Traverse

If because of the steepness of the hill or the snow and/or wax conditions you find your skis back-slipping no matter how wide you set them for your herringbone, but you think you can make faster progress than sidestepping allows, then turn both skis across the hill, angling them uphill only enough so that you

hill to keep you from sliding either downhill or sideways.

If you start slipping backward, move the tails up the hill so that they are again directly across the hill. If you start to slip forward, move the

still feel secure, and proceed to the edge of the trail. Now turn to cross the hill in the opposite direction using the kick turn (see below). Where trails are wide enough for traversing, it's an effective, energy-saving (and possibly face-saving) way to climb. Like the hiking trail that is a series of switchbacks up the side of a mountain, traversing can get you to the top, if not speedily, at least surprisingly refreshed and prepared for the wild downhill to follow.

TECHNIQUE TIP

THE KICK TURN

The kick turn is a great way to reverse direction at the end of a traverse up a steep slope or on a very narrow trail. It works in two 180-degree steps. If you're on a slope, make sure both skis are perpendicular to the fall line, that is, across the hill rather than heading down it. But please practice this turn on the flats before attempting it on a hill; it's a little tricky.

With skis across the slope, move the downhill ski slightly forward. Lift it up, tip first, and swing it all the way around for an about-face. All the while, use your poles for balance. The downhill ski is now facing the opposite direction of the uphill ski and is next to it; you're headed in two directions! Shift your weight to the ski you just turned. Before you lift up the second ski, make sure it can clear the leg you've just placed in the snow without hitting it, lifting it, or stepping on it. Mess this up now and you'll be twirled spaghetti. Swing your body and your leg around until the skis are parallel again and headed in the same direction. This is also a great way to reverse directions on a narrow trail where there is no room for a star turn.

The Traverse Sidestep

On really steep, wide hills, a combination of the sidestep and the traverse can be the secure, easy way to climb. As the name implies, you take sidesteps, but also proceed forward in a traverse, so that on each step up, one ski goes ahead. Take short steps up and short steps forward. Large steps will overextend your body and leave you prone to back-slipping or falling. You'll find traverse sidestepping quite easy and relaxing; the addition of the forward motion makes it a more natural motion than pure sidestepping.

As John Viehman demonstrates in Idaho's Sawtooth Mountains, the key to successful traverse sidestepping is to take short steps; overextending your body will lead to back-slipping and fatigue.

DOWNHILLS
AND
TURNS

Just as you need to angle your skis to climb uphill, you need to tilt something askew — either your skis or various parts of your body — to counteract the hill's fall line (the most direct distance between the spot at which you are standing and the bottom of the hill) and control both direction and speed of descent. The wedge, wedge turn, stem turn, step turn, and diagonal traverse will govern your tempo. The Telemark and parallel turns are more advanced means of negotiating steeper terrain usually associated with the back-country. Learn them on gentle gradients, and you'll feel your wilderness start to widen at every turn.

Of course, if you want to maximize your speed, there are ways to do that by keeping square to the fall line and heading for the bottom. Tuck that thought away for now.

DOWNHILL STANCE

Before you can learn any specific turn, you need to be confident about maintaining your balance going down hills. This isn't always easy for beginners. Hills are scary. As you arrive at the top of a hill, the confidence you've gained on the flats and making your way uphill suddenly gives way to the jitters, to be followed by a wave of helplessness as you start

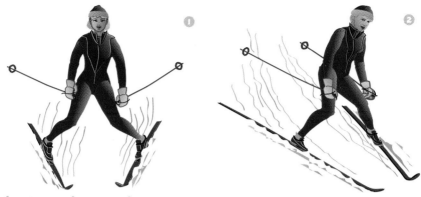

The Snowplow/Wedge Turn

1) SNOWPLOW: Push your heels out to create a V, with ski tips quite close together. Roll your ankles toward the inside edges and bend your knees toward each other.
2) SNOWPLOW TURN: For a left turn, drop your right shoulder and hand down and turn your torso to the left as you shift weight to the right ski, forcing it to carve the turn.

to accelerate down the hill and down and out. We've all felt it, but there are ways to overcome it.

First, on level ground, assume the stable downhill stance: feet 6 to 8 inches apart, weight on your entire foot and evenly balanced between your skis, knees bent, hands low and somewhat out in front of you, head up and looking forward. Now find a gentle, open bit of downhill terrain and run down it. Do it again. And again, until you're able to do so without falling. Until you're bored

with it and ready to try something a little more interesting, like controlling your speed and turning down steeper hills.

The Snowplow/Wedge

The maneuver comes with two names and many chances to use them. To slow yourself down, push out on your heels to shape your skis into an inverted V with the tips quite close together but not touching and the tails spread out to the sides. Roll your ankles toward the inside edges

---

TECHNIQUE TIP

WATER GLASS STANCE

To keep your downhill stance in line, "keep your hands in front of you as if you were carrying a tray of water-filled glasses. This will counteract the tendency to fall backward," advises Deb Ackerman, chairman of the Professional Ski Instructors of America's Nordic Education Committee.

of your skis and apply more weight on the edges to apply the brakes. Bend your knees and bring them toward each other, pushing out with both heels at the same time to control your speed. Keep your arms in front of you and your hands low to ensure proper balance. Keep your back

Applying the snowplow brakes. The wider you spread your ski tails, the slower you'll go. This skier is on the verge of stopping.

straight and your head staring down the hill.

Unweight the edges slightly if you want to increase your speed. When you want to stop, push out hard with both legs and bend the knees even more to lower your center of gravity; you don't want to resort to a face-plant to stop — better to employ your butt for that purpose if you have to. Centering your weight over the skis will keep you headed straight.

The Snowplow/Wedge Turn

A secure way to make a downhill turn, the wedge turn employs the same technique as a snowplow, except that you add weight and a twisting motion to one ski while lifting up (unweighting) the other ski. If you want to turn left, push hard on the right ski and begin to turn your torso to the left by dropping your right hand down toward your right knee. Meanwhile, take weight off the left ski. If you want to turn right, emphasize the left ski. If you want to stop altogether, simply follow the turn all the way around until you reach an uphill angle. Turning across the fall line is the most effective, secure way to stop, because when you do come to a halt, you can relax.

The Stem Turn

1) Begin the turn from a skis-together, knees-bent position traversing the hill.
2) With your weight on the downhill ski, turn your torso to face down the hill. Reach forward and down and plant your downhill pole as you begin to push out the tail of your uphill ski.
3) As you step (or stem) the uphill ski out, shift your weight over to it as it begins to turn across the fall line.
4) With weight fully shifted, the uphill (now outside) ski carves the turn.
5) It has now become the downhill weighted ski and your traverse of the hill in the opposite direction has begun.
6) Bring the new uphill ski parallel to the downhill ski and begin to turn your torso to face down the hill in preparation for the next turn.

The Step Turn

Essentially a traveling star turn, the step turn is the cross-country skier's most basic turn. It is especially useful on turns where machine-set tracks prevent you from making snowplow or stem turns. When you ski in set tracks, you'll notice that the sidewalls tend to get worn down (or even erased) when enough skiers press against their outsides on turns. The step turn is neither stylish nor graceful, but it is effective.

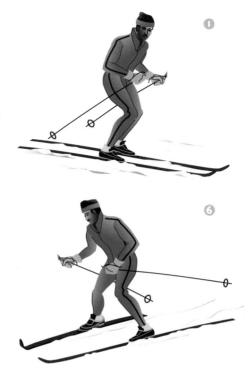

Bend your knees, keeping your weight forward and your arms in front of you. With skis parallel, pick up one ski at a time and place the tip in the direction you want to go. Then pick up the other ski and place it parallel to the first ski. Repeat this procedure with small steps, since you will be moving all the way through the turn. A large step takes your foot

TECHNIQUE TIP

KEEP YOUR TAILS DOWN

"When using the step turn, as you pick your ski tip up to place it in the direction of the turn, be sure to leave your ski tail in the snow for better balance," says Paul Peterson, coach of the Professional Ski Instructors of America Nordic Team and director of skiing at Bear Valley (California) Cross Country.

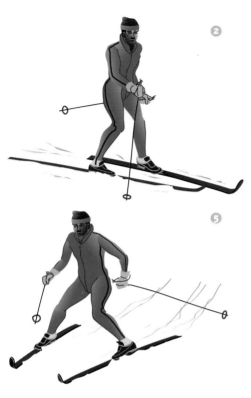

away from the snow for a longer
period of time and leaves you prone
to becoming prone.

Use your outside ski for glide,
but don't stay on it for long.
Remember, many small steps are
preferable to few big ones. Keep your
legs flexed, since straight legs tip
over more easily.

As you gain confidence and
become proficient at the step turn,
you can take large steps and push off
— as you would when you are
skating — so that you are both
turning and contributing to forward
momentum by pushing off against the
inside edge of the ski. This makes
the step turn ideal for the flats or

slight uphills where you want the
turn to keep propelling you forward.
Most turns, however, are designed to
control speed on the way down hills
by allowing you to ski back and forth
across the slope rather than speeding
straight down it.

The Stem Turn

Think of the stem turn as an aggressive snowplow, the kind that allows
you to assert yourself on packed
powder and icy surfaces.

Begin the turn from a skis-
together position traversing the hill.
With your weight on the downhill ski,
turn your upper body to face down
the hill. Reach forward and down and

The Parallel Turn

1) With skis parallel, begin by turning your head and torso down the hill and toward the direction of the turn.
2) Now reach forward and down and aggressively plant the downhill pole.
3) Use the pole plant to help unweight both skis in order to turn them.
4) Now pivot them across the fall line.
5) Having completed the turn, begin to turn your head and torso down the hill again to initiate the next turn.

plant your downhill pole as you push the tail of your uphill ski out in a semi-snowplow. In effect, you'll end up turning your body around the downhill pole.

As you step (or stem) the uphill ski out, shift your weight aggressively over to it as it begins to turn down the fall line. Weighting the uphill (or outside) ski will force it to carve the turn. You've come around and it is now the downhill, weighted ski. Bring the new uphill ski parallel to it for the next traverse across the slope. Now begin to turn your body down the hill to prepare to initiate the next turn.

The stem turn is ineffective in deep, soft snow, because the skis tend to dig into the snow and wedge themselves in as though they were crawling under a blanket. In such snow, a step turn is more prudent.

The Sideslip

Think of this as a downhill version of the sidestep. The principle is the same: Use your edges to negotiate a hill slowly while traveling sideways.

This maneuver, like the sidestep, is reserved for really steep hills. Also not-so-steep hills when you're still getting your skiing legs under you and any downhill seems a little scary.

Stand perpendicular to the hill's fall line. Lean out over your skis, but roll your knees and ankles so you can bite into the side of the hill. Relax your ankles gradually — in effect taking the breaking force off your edges — to enable you to slide down the hill. If you begin to accelerate too quickly, check your speed by turning your knees and ankles back into the hill.

ADVANCED TURNS
The Parallel Turn

You *can* parallel-turn on free-heel skis. Many novice cross-country skiers or recent converts from downhill skiing think that the parallel turn is impossible; that Telemarking is the only way to turn on cross-country skis. That's simply not the case, though the way in which you execute a parallel turn on free-heel skis dif-

fers from what you might be used to on downhill skis.

Some alpine skiers may have an advantage in applying the parallel turn to Nordic skiing, since the movements are similar to what they do each day as they descend the slopes. On the other hand, many downhillers find the transition to free-heel turns humbling. They are accustomed to relying more on their secure heels, stiff boots, and side-cut skis to do their turning for them as they aggressively cut into the snow. To perfect their turns, cross-country skiers must rely more on agility, the strength of their legs, and well-timed weight shifts.

If you can execute a good stem turn, you'll have little trouble with parallels, which are essentially stem turns without the stems. Follow most of the stem-turn drill, but keep the skis side by side throughout the turn. Parallels are especially useful in deep powder, but they also work wonderfully on packed powder, and they can be the best choice for really steep slopes.

Begin by facing the turn and planting the pole downhill. Think of an alpine slalom skier who serpentines around gate after gate. Use the plant to help unweight both skis so they are easier to swing around the pole, which acts as a fulcrum. Bend

The Telemark Turn

1-2) Midway through a left turn, your right ski is ahead and your left pole is planted.

3) The opposite arm and leg are forward as in the diagonal stride, the left knee is still down.

4) Now the left ski comes ahead and the right knee drops as the right turn is begun.

5-6) The right (downhill) pole is planted and the front ski is steering into the turn as the rear ski carves through the turn.

7) Another turn is complete; time to initiate the next left turn.

As your skis face down the hill briefly, you'll feel the sensation of having your weight awfully far back on them. Don't panic. Righting yourself will bring the rest of your body in line with your feet and prepare you for the next pole plant and the next parallel turn. Make sure that as you start to slide your skis perpendicular to the hill again — this time facing the opposite direction — you keep both skis evenly weighted. This will set you up for the next parallel turn.

your knees and drive both ski edges uphill and into the turn.

POWDER PARALLELS. In deep powder, you won't be able to edge the skis as sharply as when you cut through packed powder or older snow. To compensate for the lack of edging if the snow is soft, bend your knees as much as possible. And concentrate on centering your weight evenly over both skis. If you agressively shift weight to the downhill ski, it (and you) will take a dive. Straighten up coming out of the turn so the downhill pole plant and pivoting motion can be initiated for the next turn.

THE TELEMARK TURN

The turn named for the region of its chief proponent, Norwegian Sondre Norheim, is best known as a merry staple of backcountry revelry, so much so that the turn itself has blossomed into its own branch of adventure skiing. "I'm a Telemarker," a chap in a ski shop will say, and suddenly passersby will engage him in Telespeak about Telemark gear, Telemark trails, and Telemark teams.

Classical skiers may never need

this ambitious detour, but if you plan to stray from the Nordic center, wide-open downhill terrain is best tamed with the Telemark turn tucked away in your bag of tricks. It need not be learned, nor practiced, on Mount Everest; Mount Backyard is just as open to Teletraining.

The Telemark Stance

To make any form of Telemark turn on any surface, you need to assume the proper position. The stance is a position of safety, a starting point for Telemark turns and a great way to practice your curtsy.

Familiarize yourself with the stance on a flat surface. From an upright position with legs parallel, slide the outside (soon to be downhill) foot forward, keeping your foot flat on the ski and bending the leg at the knee to almost 90 degrees. Meanwhile, drop the knee of your trailing (inside) leg toward the heel of your lead foot. This motion, of course, brings the heel of your trailing foot well off its ski, making the Tele the one turn that only cross-country (or free-heel)

skiers can employ. Surprisingly to the novice, the success of the Telemark turn depends on keeping equal weight on both feet. You'll tend to put more weight on your lead ski, but don't; if you unweight your trailing ski, it won't carve the turn. Keep this equal weighting very much in mind, because it's difficult at first to keep equal pressure on the ski with which only the ball of your foot is in contact.

Avoid the mistake made by many beginners of adopting a fencing thrust, with the front leg bent at the knee and the back leg nearly straight, stretching out behind. This is a fine pose for Errol Flynn, not for a Teleskier.

Making the Turn

Find a slight decline with a lengthy runout for your initial Teletrials. Take one ski (let's make it your right ski for a left turn) and lead it into the turn almost as if you were assuming the snowplow position. At the same time, lightly plant your left (or downhill) pole to help initiate the turn. Keep the knee of the outside

lead leg bent in order to absorb the brunt of the turn. Bring the trailing inside ski alongside the lead ski, keeping the trailing ski flat and setting the two about midway between wedge and parallel positions, creating roughly a 30-degree angle. Remember, keep your weight evenly distributed on the two skis.

Point both knees in the direction of the turn. Then push the front and inside of your lead foot into the turn and do the same with the outside of your trailing foot, which should lift its heel off the ski as you lower your left knee toward the ground in the characteristic curtsy. Use the lead ski to steer, while the trailing ski carves through the snow, acting as part rudder, part anchor. The tip of your trailing ski should be even with and almost touching the binding of your lead ski as you begin to cross the fall line and right on through the turn.

Mid-turn in deep, steep powder. Weight your skis more evenly in such powder. Note the knee pad, vital protection from hidden rocks.

If your Telemark turn becomes insecure, you may start easing impulsively into a wedge turn. Allow yourself that fallback for a while, but as you gain confidence, you'll begin to ride out the turn as planned.

To finish the turn, undo the mechanics, uprighting your stance and bringing your skis back to parallel, and prepare to plant your right pole to initiate the turn to the right. You have now completed a single Telemark turn, the primary component for a downhill Telemark series that can take you out of the Nordic center and onto high-country slopes.

Of course, no amount of reading will teach you any of these turns. Practice will, along with some on-the-snow instruction. You may find the

TECHNIQUE TIP

PAD THOSE KNEES

Especially in soft, early-season snow, exposed logs, rocks, and other obstacles can beat up your knees. In these conditions, backcountry tourers should employ parallel techniques, which keep their knees farther off the snow than Telemark skills.

They should also invest in a good pair of knee pads if there isn't much snow on the ground. Look for pads that are reinforced, but allow you to move without restriction. Roller blade knee pads or "carpet layers' pads" are particularly effective. Don't neglect this precaution: Expert skiers have suffered fractured knee caps and worse even when wearing knee pads.

Deep powder can flummox even seasoned skiers like this one, momentarily caught off balance. He quickly recovers with a hop turn to get his skis out of the powder.

Telemark to be particularly demanding on your legs, and I recommend plenty of conditioning before setting out to master it if you are in only so-so shape.

Linking Telemark Turns

Begin the Telemark turn by edging yourself into the fall line as you would with a single Telemark turn. This time, when you stand upright,

TELEMARK OR PARALLEL

A series of Telemark turns can be very rhythmical and graceful, though very tiring, especially when you're wearing a backpack. They are most useful on the long, open slopes blanketed with thick powder snow that are associated with the backcountry of the West. Still, most Telemark skiers don't think of their favorite turn in terms of its usefulness; they just have a passion for Telemarking.

When you begin, you may have every intention of doing Telemark turns from start to finish. But on the way down, those who-are-you-kidding muscles without warning lead you instead to execute stem or parallel turns for self-preservation. This is okay. In fact, many experienced skiers rely on parallel turns for the steepest

continue back through the fall line in the other direction. If you began with a left-hand Telemark turn, you led with your right ski. Simply upright yourself, but pass through the parallel stance and lead with your left ski. Your body should now proceed in a clockwise arc. Keep the arc narrow so you can steer into the new turn more easily.

Parallel turns are best for increased stability and control on firm snow like this *sastrugi*, wind-packed snow often found at high elevations.

Always begin each turn with a rising motion into the fall line before

slopes, reserving linked Telemark turns for gentler hills. Let discretion restrict your descent to slower, less elegant turns that control speed and ultimately encourage you into perfecting a more enjoyable series of Telemark turns.

Parallels are good for increased stability and edge control on firm snow. And the turns are easier than Telemarks for people with weak legs and especially those who have knee trouble or are carrying heavy loads in their backpacks. Among other things, the parallel technique will keep your knees from dropping too low into the snow and being exposed to protruding rocks and other sharp objects along the snow cover.

The hop Telemark is the most effective Telemark technique for controlled skiing on steep terrain. Some skiers, however, prefer parallel turns on very steep slopes.

As you become comfortable with this sequence, you'll develop a noticeable rhythm: rise; lower and steer with the left knee; rise; lower and steer with the right knee. The longer you wait between turns, the wider and slower the turns will be; the less you wait, the faster and tighter they'll be.

dropping and steering your Telemark finish. As you increase your momentum, you can decrease your wedge initiation and begin to steer and edge your ski simultaneously, so you create a smooth sequence of Telemark turns.

Fine-Tuned Telemark Turns
So how do you know you've really made your (Tele)mark? Eventually, your half-wedge initiation should start to disappear and give way to turns with your torso stubbornly

TECHNIQUE TIP
PEANUT BUTTER WEDGE
To get the feel for pressing your skis into the snowplow stance, Deb Ackerman, chairman of the Professional Ski Instructors of America's Nordic Education Committee, advises that you "pretend you are spreading peanut butter with your skis as you push them into the wedge. Practice this on flat terrain before going downhill."

facing the fall line despite your legs' twisting action from side to side.

You have begun to master the Telemark turn when the following happens: One turn starts to lead into the next one so fluidly that the turning action seems like one continuous movement rather then connect-the-dots skiing; the position of your forward pole plant becomes consistent from turn to turn; you begin to edge your skis with more confidence, allowing for more speed, and are able to check the speed when necessary; you remain well balanced over the front ski, even as you apply pressure with the trailing leg; you move so smoothly and quietly that you don't even realize you're humming bars of *Sounds of Silence* during your descent.

Advanced Telemark Turns

Traditional Telemark turns require large, open spaces. Step and hop turns allow you to take on shoots and narrower trails while maintaining the capacity to change direction abruptly. If you get caught in steep terrain, it also helps to initiate the Telemark turn with either a step or jump.

STEP TELEMARK. Steer into the turn by stepping the skis from side to side as you cross the fall line. Pick up the uphill ski and move it to the outside, where it becomes the downhill ski. Be sure to step from a bent knee and bend the knee when you land, trans-

---

TECHNIQUE TIP

DEFENSIVE TELEMARK TURNS

If the idea of a Telemark appeals to you, but you're not quite ready for the speed the turn can generate, here is a simple tip you can use to help control your speed. Yes, even Telemarking has its tamer side. To learn a slower version of the turn, take off your skis and do the following exercise: Put your feet in a snowplow position and then step back with one leg to the Telemark position rather than forward as you would do if you're trying to maintain normal speed.

Once on the hill, instead of stepping or hopping forward on your lead ski, simply step or hop back with your trailing ski. Make sure the tips of the skis are equidistant on both steps. The cadence of the steps is otherwise the same. The emphasis on flexing the knees and staying low is increased. Make the trailing ski do most of the work so it acts as an anchor while the fall of the hill acts as your propulsion. This is a good way to become comfortable with the Telemark turn on a backcountry downhill.

ferring the weight to the leg that has just hit the snow. The ability to transfer weight properly that you learned on groomed, even slopes will come in especially handy during step Teles.

Never step forward; always shift the weight from side to side, and

> 66 For a man who has too much dignity, a course of Norwegian snowshoes would have a fine moral effect. Whenever you brace yourself for a fall, it never comes off. Whenever you think yourself absolutely secure, it is all over with you....But granted that a man has perseverance, and a month to spare, in which to conquer all these early difficulties, he will then find that skiing opens up a field of sport for him which is, I think, unique. 99
>
> — Sir Arthur Conan Doyle

steer the knees in the direction of the turn. Once you build some sort of up-and-down, side-to-side rhythm, you'll feel as if you're dancing on your skis. HOP TELEMARK. Compared to a step Telemark turn, the hop Tele is a speedier dance with a quicker beat. It's a cross between dancing with a hotfoot and playing hopscotch.

The hop Telemark is the most effective technique for controlled skiing in steep terrain. Edge both skis hard in order to create the platform from which to initiate the jump. Plant your poles down the hill and face the direction of the turn. Push off the platform and lead into the turn with your outside arm and shoulder.

This may seem like a contradictory instruction, but you will not swing your upper body past the point at which it is square to the fall line. You will, however, need to swivel your skis all the way around so that if they were facing left after your last landing, they are facing right after this one. To ensure that you can pull that off, pull your knees up to give them some room to crank around to their new direction. Midair turning power comes from the knees. Be sure to land with your skis parallel. Repeat the drill in the other direction and keep dancing.

THE TUCK

Now that you know how to reduce your downhill rpm's, tucking can be a fun way to gain controlled speed on moderate downhills, while conserving energy at the same time. Think of compacting yourself as though you were folding a letter. Keeping your weight on your heels, bend sharply at the waist so that your back is parallel

Telemark in deep powder. Both poles are held high in preparation for an aggressive double-pole plant before changing direction.

The downhill pole is about to be planted to initiate the new turn. The telemark turn is the best choice when carrying a backpack because it does not require jarring shifts in weight from one ski to the other.

to the ground, and bend your knees to form a 90-degree angle between thighs and calves. When you sense yourself gaining speed, you may feel the need to uncoil for greater control. In fact, the tuck is one of the most stable positions in skiing, so try holding it. What's more, the lower your rump, the closer you are to the ground and the less bothersome falling becomes.

As your confidence builds, increase your speed by lowering the tuck and trying steeper slopes. Keep your arms in front of you for balance rather than out to the side, and don't quite put your elbows on your knees. You can even interrupt the position in midtuck for a good double-pole push that will extend the slide farther as the slope flattens. Focus your eyes down the track and hold your poles so the shafts are parallel to the ground.

THE
WORLD OF
SKATING

Wouldn't it be neat if each time you learned one sport, you could utilize your expertise to master a related activity? Maybe an unrelated activity: ensemble rugby, doubles boxing, synchronized shot put, full-contact golf, and so on. Well, welcome to ski skating. Yes it's Hans Brinker and his silver. . . skis?

This hybrid blend of winter sports has been around in practice longer than synchronized anything. It dates back to the end of the last ice age. Most anyone can learn to skate on skis. If you've skated on ice, or just tried to keep warm while waiting for a bus to arrive at your street corner, you're already familiar with the to-and-fro rocking motion you use to skate on snow. Even a background in ballroom dancing will help you learn how to skate. Granted, skating is a more labor-intensive form of cross-country skiing. The added lateral motion alone dictates that you will work harder when you skate than when you use the diagonal stride. But a well-established skating rhythm will remind you of a pleasurable ride on a backyard swing combined with the greatest aerobic workout of your life. And skating is by far the fastest way to cover snow on skis.

First Strides
Don't make the mistake of trying to

The Marathon Skate

1) Gliding on your nondominant ski in the set track, having finished pushing off with your dominant ski and your poles.
2) As you bring your dominant ski forward, both poles come forward simultaneously.
3) Now you are about to double-pole plant.
4) The double-pole push is made as you push off with your dominant ski.
5) Your torso compresses to help power the pole push.
6) Your arms swing behind you in the follow-through.

The marathon skate has ancient origins, and remains the best way to get started with skating technique.

learn skating technique on classic touring skis. Skis, boots, and bindings designed for skating make all the difference. So for your first strides, go to a cross-country ski area that grooms its trails smooth and wide and rents skating equipment

(see Chapter 2 for a discussion of skating gear).

Properly outfitted, find a flat, nicely groomed spot and perform the following exercise. Stand in place, raise both poles and your dominant leg at once, and, with the stepping ski angled somewhat to the side, set them down together. Perform the exercise several more times to get a feel for the three-point balance of skating. Now take a few slow steps without gliding to familiarize yourself with the cadence. Next, plant your poles and your dominant ski with more force and let the ski glide. You've begun to skate on skis. This three-point landing and push-off is the foundation for all skating technique.

The Marathon Skate

Before the breakthrough of adjustable

poles and long before the advent of Olympic Nordic skier Bill Koch, food gatherers traveled through woods in pursuit of game wearing one short and one long ski: a small wick for propulsion and a large plank for glide. In a sense, their foresight was remarkable.

Today's skaters use wicks not much bigger than their ancient forerunners, and their marathon skating technique is the distant cousin of the food gatherers' method. The principle is the same: Use one leg to glide and the other to push off to create the glide. Because modern skaters stick exclusively to packed, groomed trails, they don't need one larger ski to float over deep snow. They can wear two identical wicks, giving them the advantage of being able to alternate assignments from leg to leg without stopping to switch skis.

Although it is losing popularity to the V-1 and other V-skating offshoots, the marathon skate is the one you'll want to learn first, since it is the least difficult and is a natural transition between diagonal striding and full-fledged skating.

YOUR STRONG SIDE. For starters, pick a dominant leg with which to push off, for most the right leg. You'll probably want to push off with your right ski all the time, leaving lefty to glide in the tracks. Use your dominant side to gain confidence with the technique, but don't get so enamored with the position that you can't switch sides. Being able to skate with your nondominant leg will reduce the burden on your dominant leg and allow you to maintain pace.

ON TRACK. As you move onto the track, slowly start gliding on the nondominant ski. With your skating ski close to your gliding ski, push off with it against the snow, edging the skating ski as you would in a herringbone step. The thrusting ski should push off at an angle just the way you push off on skates, only on skis you have the added advantage of pushing off with your poles as well. The tighter the angle between the skis, the more speed you'll generate, so be careful not to splay your kicking leg out too far.

Move your hips over the skating ski for the instant of the push and

The V-1 Skate

1) The critical three points of contact: The dominant leg and both poles hit the snow at once.
2-3) With weight shifted to the dominant (right) side, the double-pole push is completed.
4-5) The double-pole push is followed through while the glide on the dominant side continues.
6-8) Now the weight shifts to the nondominant (left) side for a glide between pole pushes. This is when the poles come forward in preparation for the next push.
9) Another strong double-pole and weight shifts again to the dominant side.
10-11) The follow-through of the pole push and the dominant side glide.

return your weight to the tracked ski for the duration of the glide.

USING THE POLES. A strong pole push is essential for propulsion. Bring the poles just short of a vertical position, taking the hands to shoulder height at the start of the push. Pull down and back, using the shoulders and upper back, compressing the torso and keeping the elbows bent until the follow-through. At that time,

allow the arms to swing behind you either at or slightly below hip height. After the follow-through, swing the arms forward again and begin raising the torso to its original erect position. Then skate on.

The V-1 Skate

This most common and versatile of all skating methods can be used on almost any groomed, untracked ter-

rain. The marathon skate may be easier to learn, and more advanced techniques may help you accelerate faster and adjust to a greater variety of terrain and conditions, but the majority of skiers who choose to skate select the V-1 as their means of locomotion.

The technique looks like a singsong series of one-legged glides and is as elegant as any activity on snow. You'll need to be able to do three things in order to skate the V-1: Shift your weight from ski to ski, balance on each ski as it glides on untracked snow, and use a double-pole push to help thrust you along after both legs have each pushed off

once. You'll also have to develop strong thigh muscles, since much of your forward motion is generated by pushing off on the inside edge of your skis with down-and-out pressure. Be sure to keep the V made by your skis as narrow as possible; a wide V sends energy off to the sides where it doesn't help propel you forward and, incidentally, takes all the grace and style out of your skating form.

STRIDING. Again you'll want to choose a dominant side, even though both legs will be pushing off with equal frequency throughout the V-1. The timings of the marathon skate and V-1 skate are similar. But when you use the V-1, your nondominant

ski remains completely unweighted; during the marathon skate, the nondominant ski remains in the track.

It's called the V-1 because you double-pole each time you skate to your dominant side, then skate without poling at all to the nondominant side, called the recovery skate. Keep your torso erect and turn it so it faces the skating ski. This will help you to keep your gliding ski flat on the snow for as long as possible

BILL KOCH TEACHES THE V-1 SKATE

Olympic silver medalist Bill Koch remains an active advocate of cross-country skiing as a healthy recreational activity. Of the technique he helped popularize, the skating pioneer says: "The V-1 is the most versatile of the many skating techniques.

"When I'm instructing students, I start by having them watch me make the V-1 movements while standing in place. In this way, they can see the critical timing of three points of contact (the dominant leg and poles) hitting the snow at the same time. They will notice that there is a complete weight shift between dominant and nondominant sides, the dominant being the three-point contact, which delivers the power of the stroke and the nondominant (gliding) phase of the stroke.

"After watching me for a few strokes, once this image is firmly planted in their minds, they join and mimic.

"After they become proficient with this three-point timing, including weight shift, then they are ready to begin stepping forward, but not yet gliding.

"Once they become proficient in keeping this timing while stepping, they simply let the dominant ski slide as a result of their full weight shift landing on it. After this full weight shift, they simply rock all of their weight back on the nondominant gliding ski.

"One way to get used to this timing is to use auditory clues. Call out your dominant side to yourself as your foot and poles hit the ground. If your right side is dominant, call out 'Right . . . Glide . . . Right. . . Glide,' being sure that there is a full weight shift with each of your calls. Poling occurs only during the dominant, power phase, in this case, when you call out the word 'Right.'

"Continue repeating these steps in this order until the timing becomes second nature."

before edging it in preparation for pushing off on it. And it centers your weight over the skating ski.

THE POLE PLANT. During the double-pole plant, think of falling forward and down with all your weight on your dominant ski and the poles. Because you will plant both poles simultaneously after every two strides, you will always plant them with your weight over the same ski. Don't expect your poles to be parallel to each other. They should both be angled backward. Similarly, the pole on that side will also be angled more sideways, with your hand lower and closer to your chest.

Compress your upper body and push down and behind you. Again, follow through, so you don't get tempted to shorten the thrust and allow the propulsion window to close. After you complete the glide of the leg on the nonpoling side, swing your arms back up in order to begin the next double-poling sequence.

DON'T HESITATE. Keep your legs moving as rhythmically as possible. Don't force yourself, but try to establish a comfortable stride pattern without any stutter steps. The more you alter the cadence of your limbs tapping against the snow, the more you are creating, in effect, man-made

This head-on view of skating reveals its dramatic side-to-side weight shifting. 1-2) The nondominant-side glide with no poling. 3) The poles come forward and up as weight shifts to the dominant side in preparation for the pole push. 4) The double-pole push, with weight fully shifted to the dominant side.

bumps for yourself, because the continuous motion will be interrupted. Remember, the muscles have to last, so you can always slow the strides, as long as they remain in a pattern that doesn't sap random bursts of energy. Also, don't rely too much on the arms, especially if you have become accustomed to double-poling on groomed tracks. The legs can always generate more force than the arms. They are your priority.

Once you've grown comfortable with the idea of double-poling over a particular ski, make sure you can continue the motion using the opposite leg. The same principle applies here as it does with the marathon skate, although the energy differential isn't as great between legs, since both are moving throughout the skating. Still, you don't want one side to grow more tired than the other.

No-pole, or free, skate: The left arm swings out over the right, or gliding, ski. By swinging your arms out over each new gliding ski you can build speed on slight downhills without planting the poles at all.

You also need to know how to make turns to both sides of your body. You will usually turn to the side of the gliding rather than striding leg. Since you'll need to turn in each direction at some point, you'll need to be able to use each flank as your poling side. Also, if the terrain is higher on your left side, you'll want to plant your poles on that side in order to compensate. If you're too dependent on poling over your right ski, the tilt in the terrain could translate to inefficient skating.

The Herringbone Skate
Also known as the diagonal V, this technique is an energy-saving means

TECHNIQUE TIP
WHICH SKATE TO USE

● The marathon skate is for use in groomed tracks, since one ski will remain entrenched at all times. It is effective on flats and gradual downhills, but is not for going uphill.

● Select the herringbone skate on steep uphills. It is the most energy-efficient, but not the fastest, means of ascent.

● The V-1, the most adaptable of the skating techniques, can be used on flats, downhill, and uphill, where it is fast but tiring.

● Use the no-pole skate as a drill for improving balance or as a transition from either the V-1 or the marathon skate as you begin the descent in an energy-conserving, speed-enhancing downhill tuck position. Or use the no-pole on slight downhills to maintain speed.

The Herringbone Skate

The simple herringbone step with some extra glide.
1) The right leg comes forward with the left pole, diagonal stride style.
2) With hips centered over the skis, weight shifts to the left ski for its glide.
3) Meanwhile the left ski and right pole move forward and up.
4) Now weight has shifted back to the left ski for its glide.

of uphill transit, particularly on steep gradients. It is less taxing than the V-1 on hills, so use the herringbone skate if you're tired.

Start the climb by doing a walking herringbone (see Chapter 4),

using the right arm with the left leg and the left arm with the right leg as you would with the diagonal stride. Think of the herringbone skate as a standard herringbone with some glide added to the end of each step.

Use all your weight and bend your knees in order to start gliding. You may need to exaggerate some of the movements in order to generate the glide necessary to carry you up the hill. That doesn't mean you should add extra strides, which will have the effect of reducing the length of the glide and defeating the purpose of using the herringbone skate in the first place. Just edge the ski more at a more severe angle to climb. Be aware that edging reduces glide, but it may be a necessary evil, depending on the hill.

Be careful not to step on your

tails, and keep your poles on the outside of your skis. Look far up the hill, so your back is forced to remain erect and you don't lean too far out over your ski tips.

The No-Pole Skate

The no-pole, or free, skate is just that: skating without using your poles. It's the preferred downhill stride among skaters. On your way down hills you may be going so fast that your poles can't keep up anyway, and you'll naturally stop poling. And on slight downhills, you can build up speed by no-pole skating.

To compensate for the lack of pole plants, your arms should swing out farther forward and even slightly across your body toward the tip of the opposite, or gliding, ski. Picture the upper-body motion of speed skaters. But be careful not to get carried away and swing your arms so far that your torso is following around, sending momentum side to side rather than straight ahead.

Use the same mechanics as you learned in the V-1, and be sure to keep your weight centered over the flat gliding ski. Don't allow your body to sink into the gap between the skis. Keep a reasonably compressed V shape. The greater the angle of the skis and the more distance you have to travel from ski to ski, the less transferable your weight will be.

Besides helping you maintain and build speed down hills, the no-pole skate can also sharpen your sense of balance and reinforce your capacity to glide on one leg.

The Skate Turn

Think of a skate turn as a more forceful version of the step turn. The entrance into both turns is identical. But instead of making defensive steps that reduce your speed and emphasize control, you'll be edging your skis and flexing your legs for a more dynamic push off the outside ski. If you are turning to the left, push off decisively with the right ski.

Herringbone skating in tandem up a slight hill. Be careful not to cross your ski tails, keep your poles outside your skis, and look far up the hill to avoid slouching.

Start by moving your body in the direction of the turn and creating a forceful push off the outside ski that shifts your weight over the inside ski. If only for the sake of balance, you may want to include a pole plant. A double-pole push will further increase your speed. Double-pole over the outside ski. Then, after what will probably be an abbreviated follow-through, swing your arms back over the inside ski. Depending on the size of the arc of the turn, you may want to repeat the process.

There is nothing more graceful on skis than accomplished skating. This skier is no-pole skating and is in the midst of a turn.

ADVANCED TECHNIQUES

That's not all, folks. There are more refined techniques available to skaters, the technical applications of which are better left to your career as the Bill Koch of the next generation. In the span of a decade, the centuries-old methods of skating that hadn't necessarily been categorized as such and certainly hadn't been generally accessible to the skiing populace have become such a collage of step-edge-glide-and-pole blueprints it's difficult to know what the skate-of-the-art will look like a week from Thursday.

The V-2 Skate

Believed to be the fastest, most taxing means of skating, the V-2 incorporates two double-pole pushes for every completed V-skate, or simply one double-pole push for each stride and weight transfer onto one ski.

The V-2 Alternate

Developed by Swedish cross-country legend Gunde Svan as a way to maintain speed without compromising control as he'd have to do if maintaining the V-1 on certain flats and moderate downhills, the V-2 alternate skate incorporates one double-pole push for every completed V-skate and looks the way a large LP used to sound when played at 45 rpm. The skating and poling phases are specifically timed, yet unsynchronized.

The Jump Skate

Infrequently called the V-3, this incorporates a double-pole plant followed by a jump followed by a double ski skate. If somebody gave you a hotfoot, you could do this.

V-1 skaters in triplicate. The side-to-side sway of the step is akin to dancing.

BACKCOUNTRY SKIING

Just what is "backcountry skiing"? The answer depends on who you ask and where he or she lives. Ask someone from Colorado, and you hear of high-country backcountry, masses of fresh powder covering wide-open, miles-long mountain meadows, linked Telemark turns down thousands of vertical feet, week-long hut-to-hut tours from Vail to Aspen. Ask an Easterner, and you hear tales of skiing a hair-raising stretch of Vermont's Catamount Trail, or daylong trips on farm lanes and abandoned woods roads, or treks up frozen stream courses deep into the otherwise impenetrable Maine woods. The experiences are as different as

the terrain, the quality of the snow, and, some would argue, the skiers themselves. But backcountry skiers have one characteristic in common: They make their own tracks. They leave behind the groomed and patrolled tracks of the Nordic center and light out on a far less predictable, more adventurous sort of skiing where all the skills they've honed on set tracks and some new inventions as well come into play as they discover a world that only fellow cross-country skiers can know.

Touring the backcountry can mean buying specialized skis, boots, and bindings to embark on ambitious outings into the mountains, where

Backcountry skiers make their own tracks far from Nordic centers where they find a world that only fellow cross-country skiers can know.

and taken for granted most of the year but, without skis, was inaccessible all winter. Come to think of it, plenty of remote country that only determined bushwhackers can experience in summer are wide open to cross-country skiers once several feet of snow have erased the underbrush.

Backcountry experiences — large and small — are not easily forgotten. Whether it's an afternoon spent exploring logging roads on the ridge behind your house or a hut-to-hut trek, expect the unexpected, be prepared, and be self-sufficient so you can enjoy yourself to the fullest. Read Chapter 9, on safety, very closely, since all of the advice pertains to the backcountry and some pertains exclusively to skiing in the backcountry.

Never ski beyond your ability,

touring is really a means to an end. Mountain tourers will don skins and climb to great heights purely for the joy of linking Telemark turns back down. But it can also mean exploring your own neighborhood on the same touring skis you've been using all along. In fact, for many cross-country skiers, the sport has always meant just that: skiing across country — whatever country was close at hand

and when you are skiing deep into the backcountry, go with an experienced guide or someone who has done what you're going to do many times before. While skis and snow provide the means to head off into remote regions, winter conditions also provide the ingredients of sudden disaster. It doesn't take long for hypothermia or frostbite to set in should something go wrong, and the fact that you're in trouble only a mile from your back door doesn't make 10°F feel any warmer. Never underestimate the elements. Always wear (or carry) more clothing than you think you need. And carry some food and plenty of water, even for a morning outing.

Some advise against going out alone, but the most transforming moments on skis can occur in solitude. So take extra precautions if you go alone. Tell someone where you're going, when you are departing, and when you expect to return. Then follow through by letting that person know you have returned safely. And do not go alone on anything more than a day tour; winter camping is not a solo sport.

BACKCOUNTRY BASICS

How to get started as you seek to ski off beyond the groomed trails of your Nordic center? Ironically, with your Nordic center. Its owners and instructors are avid skiers who assuredly have explored every mile of skiable terrain in your neighborhood. Seek their advice. And get in touch with a local skiing or outing club. Such groups are great sources of local knowledge. Their members have sought out the hiking trails and woods roads best suited to cross-

66 When I do things on skis, I don't do them to show off—and I usually do them alone. I don't like to ski with other people because I don't want to be conscious of them. I don't want to be worried about being behind them or ahead of them. Skiing gives me a terrific sense of freedom—and I would define freedom as not having to be around other people. 99

—Truman Capote

country skiing, and would welcome you on one of the day tours they lead.

Think about the sort of terrain you want to ski. If you want to head into the mountains, planning and route-finding will occupy you long before you set off on skis. Just as you prepare for day hikes and overnight backpacking trips, so you must prepare for backcountry skiing. Yet early trips away from Nordic centers needn't take you into uncharted wilderness. Many local and state

A winter camper plans his route for the day's skiing from the shelter of an igloo, Sawatch Range, Rocky Mountains in central Colorado.

situation. But the better you learn the techniques on easier surfaces and the more you venture into different backcountry venues, the better equipped you'll be to safely enjoy the diversity of skiing experiences that only the backcountry can offer.

parks and even national forests offer detailed maps of cross-country routes where you can get away from Nordic center crowds and groomed tracks, yet still follow well-marked trails or forest roads. If you want to venture farther afield, consult local guidebooks, either ones designed for skiers or those written for hikers.

Techniques are not as preordained in the backcountry as they are on the controlled environs of groomed trails. When conditions change at every turn, you may find yourself using a sideslip here, a skid there, a stem christie followed by a hop Telemark followed by a move you may never have tried before and wouldn't be able to duplicate again. *What's that? That's my get-around-the-tree turn. How does it work? Haven't a clue.*

The rule in the backcountry isn't always to use perfect form in every

Breaking Trail

Being the first person to ski through pristine snow teaches certain lessons you'll never learn on groomed tracks. One such is how to break trail. And having said some memorable backcountry moments are solo ones, it must be added that breaking trail through deep or wind-packed powder or wet snow is memorable for all the wrong reasons. It's outright exhausting. The key to breaking trail through such snow is numbers — numbers of skiers.

When you aim to cover a long distance and the snow is deep or wet, always ski with a group of friends so that you can change off lead skiers regularly. When a lead skier begins to feel fatigued (but before he is truly flagging), he simply stops, sidesteps off his tracks, and lets the next skier

For longer outings into the backcountry, pulling gear on a *pulk,* a Scandinavian sled designed for the purpose, can be preferable to a backpack, which can put too much weight over the skis.

pull into the lead, waiting for the last skier to pass by before sidestepping back into the now nicely broken track. Ah! What a relief. Leapfrogging in this manner also ensures that everyone has a chance to lead, preventing the strongest skiers from hogging the lead and setting too fast a pace. Maintaining the right pace is critical; in a group, the pace should

Breaking trail through deep or packed powder is exhausting. Leapfrogging — regularly changing off lead skiers — is the way to go.

that provide better flotation, a larger wax packet for more grip, and better overall maneuverability.

Trail Skiing

Skiing uncharted terrain can mean striding across wide-open rolling meadows or Telemarking down equally spacious high-country bowls. It can mean tooling along generous, gently graded national forest roads. But, particularly in the East, it more often means navigating very narrow, steep, winding trails designed for hiking, or no trail at all but the one you make by weaving back and forth between trees. Called by some "survival skiing," this can be the truest test of nerve and your ability to improvise. Survival skiing is not about showing off conventional form or style. It is about resorting to whatever works. Sometimes trails are so narrow that there isn't even room enough for the old standby snowplow. The only way to get down is to tuck and either drag your poles or fall down to check your velocity. So be prepared, exercise caution, and be willing to gamble occasionally. Here are a few tips for safely engaging in survival skiing. For the most part, though, you're on your own.

POLE STRAPS OFF, GOGGLES ON. Catching the basket of your ski pole on the underbrush that encroaches narrow trails is a wrist-wrenching way to stop unexpectedly. Before descending a narrow, tree-lined trail or through evergreen groves, remove

be set by the slowest skier.

Don't try to maintain the long, gliding diagonal stride you pride yourself in on groomed trails. Your stride as you break trail through deep snow is more akin to walking or to the short, shuffling stride you use on hills. As when climbing, you want maximum grip to help you plow forward in relatively small steps. And you will find yourself relying more on your poles and upper body if the going is steep and the snow is deep. Breaking trail in such conditions for long on touring skis will begin to convince you of the advantages of wider, shorter backcountry-style skis

your pole straps. Far better to have to retrace your tracks to retrieve a snagged pole than to ski out with a dislocated shoulder.

There are times when you'll have your straps off anyway, to employ the unglamorous but effective pole drag, in which you drag both poles to your side to brake your descent.

Wear glasses or goggles to protect your eyes from tree boughs, and be prepared to perform sudden tucks more akin to squats to avoid low branches.

STAGGERED STARTS. Don't closely follow the leader down a steep, narrow trail; give him an ample head start to avoid a pileup. Waiting for the skier ahead also allows him to give you some idea of what's ahead, either by shouting out warnings or through body language: a crumpled heap with skis flailing.

THE SIT STOP. Among cross-country skiers, falling is always OK (see Chapter 3). On narrow trails, it can be mandatory. Forget about your pride and fall plenty. On long narrow downhills where there is no room to turn, falling can be the only way to check your speed and proceed safely. Just give in and get used to the idea of purposefully sitting back on your butt to one side of your skis and stopping, only to get up again and do it all over. The alternative could well be a knee-twisting encounter between ski tip and underbrush or a head-on encounter with a tree. Doesn't falling sound like a sensible alternative?

HIGH-COUNTRY BACKCOUNTRY

An instructor in an Outward Bound course once offered this mantra: "Good judgment comes from experience and experience comes from bad judgment." Apply the principle to skiing in any remote area, but particularly to the serious backcountry of the Rocky Mountains and the Far West. This is country where many backcountry skiers head out with the specific aim of climbing up mountains to enjoy the long runs back down through deep powder. This is where local knowledge is essential, conditions can get nasty very quickly, and avalanche danger can be real.

Before heading off toward the high peaks, start on little hills or perhaps on some downhills at alpine resorts, where the terrain is carefully managed. Ski with someone more experienced than you, but not someone who will show off and goad you into skiing beyond your ability. Don't allow yourself to get so comfortable with a limited number of techniques that you exclude others from your repertoire entirely. Practice repetitions until the techniques become instinctive rather than planned.

We have covered all the basic techniques you need in earlier chapters. Before tackling the backcountry you should have mastered them. What's different in the backcountry? For one thing, you are likely to find steeper slopes than you thought possible.

Steep Slopes

Don't feel you're wimping out if you bag the deep drops. Some find living on the edge to be exhilarating. For others, worry, even unnecessary worry, takes the fun out of activities that should be fun. You don't have to ski down a hill just because it's there. Challenge yourself, but do it safely, and if you don't enjoy a particular challenge, try another slope. Once

> 66 To be skiing is to be in a world not of man, but of light — an alternation of sun and shade, sparkling, evanescent, existing only in the moment. 99
>
> —Morten Lund

you choose a slope, you need to be aggressive with it. Timid skiers who lack confidence tend to keep their legs very rigid, so they are less likely to bend their knees properly and more likely to fall. If you don't feel confident enough to be aggressive, try an easier hill.

Above all, bear in mind that most avalanches occur on 30-to-45-degree slopes. Always check with local sources regarding avalanche conditions.

Once you decide to descend a steep drop, never be afraid to employ those survival skiing skills you have at your disposal. The best back-country skiers are those with a penchant for invention but also a healthy respect for terrain and conditions. As you size up the drop, keep three points in mind: the angle of the slope, the type of snow, and the types of downhill technique you have at your disposal to safely, comfortably cope with the slope.

More experienced skiers — or those with blind confidence — will go for the fall line and, as their speed rapidly increases, adjust their turns, making them more aggressive and frequent. They may employ a hybrid Tele-parallel turn that allows for closer, faster turns to control acceleration. Or they may just stick with parallel turns, the preferred way to keep acceleration under control on steep drops. Many skiers who are just getting comfortable on more difficult slopes may find the parallel stance more stable than the more vulnerable position of the Telemark. Parallels are also a smart choice on shallow, early-season snow, where Telemark turns, with their low knee bends, would expose your knees to protruding rocks.

But there are other alternatives for the less confident, such as taking your sweet time with a series of long, diagonal traverses back and forth

Ski mountaineer, Detroit Plateau, Danco Coast, Antarctic Peninsula. Deep, steep powder like this calls for advanced skills that can only be gained through long experience.

Jewel Basin, Montana. Crust and crud makes for challenging skiing. On steep slopes, many skiers use a hop-parallel turn to maintain control.

across the slope. Each traverse can end in a parallel turn or even a kick turn. And don't forget about the snowplow, that safe, stable, in-control way to negotiate the toughest downhills. Even experienced backcountry mountain skiers fall back on it when they're feeling pressured by fatigue and extreme slopes.

Deep Powder

Knee-deep, Western powder is an ideal dreamed about by many skiers who have yet to visit the Rocky Mountains, where it is the rule rather than the exception. But for those who haven't grown up with this ideal, it can pose surprising challenges. Of course, the only way to learn about its unique qualities is to ski it. But a few

observations will help prepare you.

First of all, this is where the new lighter, shorter, wider Tele and mountaineering skis truly excel, so if you're going to ski powder for the first time, don't bother experimenting with traditional skinny touring skis. Get some wide skis, whether you buy or rent. They'll make everything else about powder easier and a lot more fun.

That's primarily because their greater surface area helps you float on and over the powder rather than sink down into it. And floating has to do with the key modification you'll need to make in your technique: Keep your weight evenly balanced over both skis, even on turns. The aggressive edging and weight shifting that turning across the fall line on

packed powder or crud requires will leave you mired in deep powder.

The Telemark turn is ideal for deep powder, so it's no surprise that it is the only turn — aside from the snowplow — in which your weight is evenly distributed. But there are times when you'll want to parallel-turn in powder. That, too, is perfectly possible if you can get out of the habit of weighting your downhill ski. Think of turning on powder as a chance to use finesse rather than force.

Crust and Crud

Leave a frosted cake uncovered overnight and what do you have? A thin, hard, crackly layer of frosting over an extra-mushy thicker under-layer. Backcountry terrain can be just like that. It isn't always as definable as ice-covered slush, but the variable layers can make the approach to any descent positively puzzling and phys-ically demanding.

In these conditions, it is some-times easier to get your feet off the snow to make your turns. An exag-gerated jump will extract you from getting some part of your ski caught underneath the ice cover as it sinks into the soup. You may want to add an extra hop or jump to your Tele-mark and parallel techniques. On a breakable, hard, chippy surface, skis

---

10th MOUNTAIN HUT SYSTEM

With 54 standing huts, Colorado has the most huts of any state in the United States. Its flagship system is the 10th Mountain Hut System, the best-known of all such systems in the United States. Orig-inally intended as a way to con-nect the Colorado towns of Vail and Aspen, it consists of 10 huts and was named for the U.S. Army's 10th Mountain Division, a unit of 15,000 accomplished skiers, climbers, and adventurers that saw significant action in Italy's Dolomites during World War II.

The soldiers underwent training in skiing, mountaineering, and alpine survival while sta-tioned at Camp Hale near the Ten-nessee Pass. The division helped to drive Nazi forces from the Po Valley in Italy.

When the victorious troops returned, Fritz Benedict and Pete Siebert, two soldiers who were Aspen natives, designed the now-famous resort town of Vail. Bene-dict envisioned a hut system that would one day connect the two towns. In 1979, Benedict skied the European system joining Zer-matt, Switzerland, with Chamonix,

continued on next page

France, site of the inaugural Olympic Winter Games in 1924. He used the European prototype to help design the 10th Mountain hut system on much of the public land he once used for training. Today, many of the huts have been named in memory of a division soldier or a soldier's family member. The first completed hut was named for Margaret McNamara, deceased wife of Robert McNamara, former U.S. Secretary of Defense, who supported the project from its inception. The huts are separated by an average of 5 to 7 miles, and the system is designed so that skiers of intermediate ability can ski from hut to hut in one day.

The system never quite reached Vail on its own, although the 10th Mountain is now linked with two other privately owned systems. The entire network comprises 22 trails over 300 miles of land stretching beyond both Vail and Aspen.

will slip easily, so make sure you crunch them into the soft snow below. Exaggerate your jump so you can punch through the top layer and get back out of the undermoosh. This is very physical, tiring skiing in which you are working to overpower the snow.

In the West above treeline, you may encounter wind-tortured, hard-packed snow with ridges called *sastrugi*. Here quick, aggressive parallel turns are the answer.

Ice

Sometimes the best solution when you encounter ice is to avoid it. Be aware that many ice patches — as opposed to obvious creeks and streams — are simply slick chunks of terrain surrounded by hardpack. If you notice, say, a 20-foot-long ice surface ahead, try to relax and just zip straight over it rather than attempting to stop or slow down. If you encounter a long stretch of ice, consider removing your skis and walking.

SKIING WITH A BACKPACK

The first rule of combining a backpack with skis is to keep your pack as compact and light as possible to give your arms plenty of room to swing. That means always carrying just enough, but not too much. For extended trips when a full-size pack is required, it means choosing an internal-frame backpack over an

external-frame one. An internal-frame pack carries weight low and close to your body, giving you greater stability on your skis. And its lower profile also ensures plenty of clearance for your arms to swing freely.

Back-packers carry mostly stuffed clothing that is more bulky than it is heavy. For this reason, packs are usu-ally classified not by how much weight they can accommodate, but by volume (in cubic inches).

A pack for every purpose. 1) A fanny pack should follow you everywhere, even on half-day outings. It can carry the essentials: wax, water, a snack, and an extra jacket. 2) Small day packs can accommodate the essentials plus lunch, map and compass, and more clothes. 3) Large day packs include handy side pockets plus straps for a shovel. 4) Expedition packs are meant for multi-day trips and have space enough for tent, sleeping bag, cook stove and a full complement of clothing.

The variations include fanny packs, which actually fit around the waist and run between 450 and 800 cu. in.; small day packs, running from 1,200 cu. in. and 2,500 cu. in. and supporting between 5 and 10 pounds; large day packs, which are probably the most common carrier in the backcountry, running between 2,600 and 3,600 cu. in. and supporting between 12 and 20 pounds; overnight packs, running between 3,600 and 5,000 cu. in. and carrying up to 35 pounds; and expedition packs, running as large as 8,000 cu. in. and accommodating up to 100 pounds, perfect if you plan to climb Mount McKinley, but more than most recreational skiers care to lug.

Fanny Packs

Often worn by distance runners or people doing light hiking, these ultralight waist packs are good for half-day tours or even strolls around the Nordic center. Stuff a water bottle, some ski wax, a candy bar, and possibly an unlined windbreaker inside and you've filled it to capacity.

Small Day Packs

These include larger belt packs and very light backpacks. Perhaps you're planning a half-day tour with a stop for lunch or on a day with changing weather conditions that requires you to carry multiple clothing options. The belt packs and light backpacks can both support more substantive snacks, a map and compass, a water bottle or thermos, and perhaps a Gore-Tex jacket or an extra pile sweater to accommodate the variable conditions.

Large Day Packs

As you move up in volume, you find packs with more sophisticated suspension systems — in essence, more padding. Most big day packs come with closed-cell-foam padding along the back and bottom of the pack that help to vent sweat away from your back. Some designs have padding molded with undulating grooves that allow air to move between the foam and your back. This doesn't prevent you from sweating more on your weighted back than your unweighted front, but it does reduce some of the moisture as well as keeping objects with corners or rough edges from digging into you. Most large day packs include side compartments for waxes, water bottles, or a small camera.

Overnight Packs

Good for skiing to and from huts or for carrying large day loads, these packs hold a sleeping bag, clothing changes, insulated jackets or vest, an optional spare sweater, and the food you'll need to prepare breakfast and dinner. Packs this size and larger should have a reinforced bottom and a narrow frame with compression straps that can slightly alter the shape of the pack. Remember, if you're double-poling, you don't want your elbows running into your pack. Again, stick with internal-frame models.

Expedition Packs

The largest packs are good for multi-day winter trips and excursions to faraway destinations. Professional photographers who need to carry 15 to 20 pounds of photo equipment might carry a pack like this, unless they prefer to have a belt pack specifically dedicated to camera gear, though this can be cumbersome.

A ski guide or group leader, responsible for carrying certain items the others may not need, might want a pack this size. A group of eight can do with one stove, a few pots, a fuel supply, a flashlight, and one or two of many other things.

Packing into the mountains often means carrying your skis. Climbing such heights in winter can be reward enough, but the run back down is the ultimate reward.

Added Features

High-end overnight packs may include such amenities as a top flap that acts as a handy map pocket, clips on the inside of the pocket made to store a set of hut or car keys, and even a vertical flap on the pack's exterior that can carry a shovel or your skis if you are combining snowshoeing with skiing. You can also stick skis or snowshoes inside your pack's compression straps and tighten the straps around them.

Some large day packs and most overnight and expedition packs have shoulder straps, waist straps, and varied frame shapes that can accommodate different-sized people who may carry the same materials in their packs. There is also a wide range of sizes, including models designed for the contours of a woman's build. If you're buying a small day pack, one or two sizes are meant to fit all.

How to Pack and Ski

People who are only used to packing suitcases may not appreciate the skill involved in stuffing a backpack. Remember, you'll need to dip into it frequently during your journey, including times when you're out in the cold and have neither the patience nor the circulation to fiddle around for what you packed first, need most, and can't reach because it's on the bottom.

If you're packing for an overnight

A ski-mountaineer in full regalia, Mount McKinley expedition. Sleds are best suited to wide-open, relatively flat terrain. They can be adapted to carry young children on less ambitious outings.

your back, where they'll help keep the pack's center of gravity in line with yours, and prevent it from becoming tippy.

Snack and lunch foods — trail mix or a power bar you may need for quick energy — should be more accessible than breakfast and dinner foods that you eat in your hut.

Keep a top flap or readily accessible compartment available for a first aid kit (see page 137). Before any stage of every journey, make absolutely cer-

stay, stash the items that you know won't be needed until you reach your hut at the bottom. This includes your sleeping bag, and extra clothes you may wear only at night or on a subsequent day.

Pack heavy items like extra water bottles, thermoses, extra food, and pots down inside and close to

tain you can get to what you might need in an emergency. Your water bottle is your next priority, followed by snack food, ski waxes or skins, and map. Some top flaps detach and can double as belt packs, a handy option if you decide to go for a quick early-morning tour once you've reached your shelter.

Tighten hip belts to reduce the pack from swaying and placing an extra burden on your shoulders when you double-pole. You may want to shorten your poles when you ski with a pack, simply because you won't be swinging your arms as much as you would without one. When you ski, take shorter strides and concentrate on keeping yourself centered.

SLEDS

Faced with the option of carting 80 pounds on their back, some people prefer to carry a 40-pound pack and pull a 40-pound sled. Such sleds, or *pulks*, have a molded fiberglass body with a nylon cover. The gear sits in the bottom, and the nylon top half fits on the fiberglass, creating a weather-proof cover. Two aluminum tubes, or stays, roughly 5 to 6 feet long, connect the front of the sled to a padded hip belt much like those on back-packs.

The sleds are good because they enable you to place some of the weight burden on the snow. If you've dragged a suitcase along rollers as you walk through an airport, you know how much easier it can be than to carry the suitcase. Sleds take some getting used to, because they tend to pull you backward when you're going uphill and they can make negotiating narrow turns challenging. They're best suited to the wide-open, relatively flat terrain of regions of the Midwest. They're not the right choice

for threading through fairly dense stands of trees or where you are looking forward to Telemarking down long hills.

HUT-TO-HUT SKIING

Huts are catching on in a big way in the United States. Long a favored form of alpine accommodation in Europe, huts have been slow to win converts in America, but that is changing rapidly. In just three seasons, from 1991 to 1993, Colorado's 10th Mountain Hut System (see sidebar, pages 113-114) saw a three-fold increase in use. In the 1993 – 94 season the system booked 30,000 hut user reservation nights.

Why the sudden surge in interest? There are probably several reasons, one of which is a desire to strike out and experience the high mountain backcountry and get away not only from Nordic ski areas, but also from the predictable grind and expense of downhill resorts. And it may have something to do with more skiers reaching an age where they want the adventure and awe-inspiring beauty of the backcountry, but none of the uncertainty and discomfort of winter camping. For them, the security of hut-to-hut skiing is ideal. And at a cost of around $25 a night, it is also a bargain. For many, hut-to-hut is the ultimate all-around experience, with classic Nordic touring, access to superb powder slopes and glades, and everywhere breathtaking scenery.

It's a wonder hut-to-hut skiing wasn't discovered sooner.

This inexpensive and serviceable form of lodging consists of permanent or semipermanent shelters designed for day or overnight use by backcountry travelers. "Hut" is a generic term for all backcountry shelter; it includes wood-sided cabins, log cabins, yurts, expansive lodges, even converted mining buildings. Huts have a long tradition in Europe, where many huts are, in fact, huge lodges that can house up to 300 or 400 skiers. People are there to cook for you, clean up after you, and act as ski guides. In North America, huts are generally far smaller and almost universally self-serve.

The Gates Hut, one of 10 huts in the renowned 10th Mountain Hut System that links the towns of Vail and Aspen, Colorado.

What You'll Find

Overnight visitors use huts equipped with beds, pillows, perhaps blankets — bring a sleeping bag or ask the hut director, to be safe — a propane stove for cooking, a wood-burning stove for heating and melting snow for water, a fuel supply, plates, and pots and pans. Huts for day travelers generally have some chairs, a few tables, and a stove to melt some water. Some are provisioned with canned foods and the like.

YURTS. A yurt is a single-walled or rubberized circular tent with full hut amenities. It usually has a sturdy alu-

minum frame or a solid wood frame. What sets yurts apart is their portability. Huts and cabins are permanent by definition; yurts are usually on a platform that can be disassembled, making them transportable.

What You Won't Find

You must, of course, furnish your own water. Unless you find the odd facility with a well on the premises or bring enormous supplies of bottled water, this means melting snow that has fallen near the hut. For this reason, users should respect the cleanliness of the hut area. Take out what you bring in, garbage included. Do not leave uneaten food in whatever basket or garbage bag the hut

A yurt in the San Juan hut system in southern Colorado provides snug accomodation and all the amenities of a permanent hut.

North American huts.

Cost

Small huts, generally classified as yurts, housing four to eight people, usually run between $70 and $140 a night for a group. In larger huts, the fees normally apply on a per-person basis. These huts often house from 12 to 18 people in lengthwise bunks that run in tiers along the walls. The charge can run as low as $15 and rarely exceeds $30. In larger huts you will often be lodged with other groups, especially on weekends and during the peak season.

Some huts are provisioned with canned foods, but you should be prepared to pack in much of your own food and to pack out everything you brought. Here, John Viehman prepares for a tour of Idaho's Sawtooth Mountains.

provides, and do not throw any refuse outside the door expecting it to disappear in time for the next group of hut visitors. Dogs, even guide dogs, are not allowed near the huts. Most huts are also constructed in areas where there are few signs of wildlife during the winter months.

Most toilet facilities are crude — usually outhouses — and huts don't come with shower facilities unless they are constructed near a reservoir, are powered by solar heat, or are part of a lodge with a sizable generator. Showers are almost never available in

For more details on hut-to-hut opportunities, see Sources & Resources.

C L O T H I N G

Your skis, boots, and poles are in place. That's the hard part. Clothing, stuff to keep you warm — that you know about. Been wearing it your whole life. No problem. Sure it's freezing, but your down coat is blizzard-worn and battle-tested. You're set. Trouble is, after two strides on skinny skis, you feel as though you're sweating in a straitjacket.

Lesson learned, you return with T-shirt and sweatshirt, perhaps a windbreaker as well. You are moving unencumbered, feeling smart and enjoying the peculiar sounds of winter. A woodpecker? An ovation? No, just your teeth chattering.

This trial-and-error exercise leaves you pessimistic of ever being dexterity-wise without becoming circulation-foolish. But it can be done.

Modern clothing is a vastly researched microclimate management system around your body. By adopting a flexible layering system that utilizes proper materials, you can insulate yourself without restricting your movement, and keep moisture — yours and Mother Nature's — away from your skin.

Cotton Is Rotten

Almost no fabric clings to perspiration as insistently as cotton. A cotton T-shirt, for instance, will soak your body in your own steaming sweat.

Then, as the cold air hits, you'll think you've stepped out of the shower and into a refrigerator. Oh, for a gust of mid-July around that next turn. Something as seemingly harmless as an added undershirt can ruin good choices of outer layers. Avoid blue jeans, too. When waterlogged, they'll remind you of sponges. When waterlogged and then frozen, they'll remind you of armor.

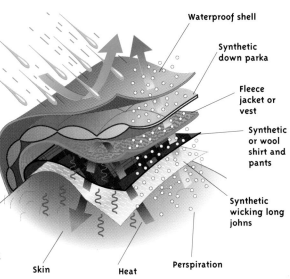

Layering in Winter

Waterproof shell

Synthetic down parka

Fleece jacket or vest

Synthetic or wool shirt and pants

Synthetic wicking long johns

Skin

Heat

Perspiration

The Law of Layering

Here is one of the few immutable laws of comfortable, safe cross-country skiing: Never wear one heavy article of clothing when two lighter ones can be worn instead. Wearing multiple layers of varying thickness allows you to regulate your body temperature, so that you can peel off layers when you're skiing all-out and then replace those same layers when you stop to rest and rehydrate. Layering allows you to respond to your body's requirements, keeping it warm, but not too hot; cool, but not chilly. Besides, layering keeps you warmer than one thick layer, because air is trapped — and warmed — between each layer as well as within each layer.

THE BASE LAYER. Your primary cover is essential for efficient insulation. We're talking more than long underwear here. The base layer should cover you all the way from neck to toe. Wear a polypropylene — or to be even more comfortable, one of the newer synthetic blends like Thermax, Polar Fleece, or Capilene — base layer that stretches to fit your contours. Lycra blends are especially stretchy and comfortable. All of these synthetic fabrics, unlike cotton, wick moisture away from your skin to keep you drier and warmer.

Capilene and other synthetic underwear come in lightweight, mid-weight, and expedition-weight. Use the lightweight for cross-country skiing and any activity that demands sustained activity. Use midweight in

colder conditions or when you plan to winter-camp or otherwise spend inactive time out in the cold. Expedition-weight underwear should be reserved for severe cold or Arctic environs and/or used as a lightweight, midweight, or insulating layer over lighter layers.

Two words of caution. Used polypro attire has all the aromatic integrity of yesterday's poached eggs. Wash liberally, but don't tumble-dry unless you plan to shrink, too. The newer synthetic blends and contemporary polypro have fewer shortcomings than early generations of polypro — they won't stink or shrink, because their synthetic properties are more advanced — but they are also more expensive. Prepare to pay several times more for these fabrics than you would for your cotton long underwear, but don't be penny-wise and goose-bump-foolish. Several extra dollars are not a high premium for comfort in the cold.

THE INSULATOR LAYER. Virtually all of the thicker fleeces and piles represented in layering's middle tier are manufactured by the same company and sold under different brand names. Polar Plus and Polar Fleece are soft, fuzzy fabrics that come in varying thicknesses. Thinner versions are usually a blend of fleece and Lycra. If you're whipping around a touring center, lightweight fleece will be fine. Like Capilene and other synthetic underwear, insulating fleeces are designed to wick moisture away from the body. They are not designed to block chilly winter winds, which is where the outer layer comes in.

THE SHELL LAYER. Somebody has to straight-arm the elements. Think of the shell as your body's lead blocker, an All-Pro breathable outer garment. If your itinerary is brief on a warm, early-season day, you may be fine with just the first two layers, but carry a shell in case the weather turns.

Most high-end shell garments are made with Gore-Tex, a waterproof, breathable laminate that works like the membrane of human skin. The

How Gore-Tex Works

The microscopic holes in the Gore-Tex laminate allow tiny perspiration droplets to escape, yet are so small they keep raindrops out.

— Polyester or nylon shell

— Gore-Tex laminate

— Lining

The right clothing — including synthetic underwear followed by an insulator layer and topped off with a protective shell layer — will keep you smiling even when it's cold enough to make your breath freeze.

aware that backpacks will throw off the equation, because they create a heavy weighted layer on only one side of you. Until the advent of the Gore-Tex Funkyvest, there is no way to prevent your back from sweating more than your front. This makes proper layering even more vital.

A down coat or heavy sweater may also come in handy après ski, but only when you don't have to ski with it. The insulating properties of down will break the wind, but can also absorb moisture, leaving you wet and weighted. And down is simply too warm to wear for long when you're exerting yourself. Other modern synthetics that work better when you're exercising or in humid conditions include Polarguard, LifeLoft, PrimaLoft, and MicroLoft.

On warm days when you don't want too much insulation, you can also wear a light windbreaker over

laminate is a Teflon-treated material that acts as a one-way valve. Its pores — 9 billion per square inch — are smaller than water droplets, but larger than the water vapor produced by your body. The shell escorts your moisture away while keeping rain and snowflakes from entering. The shell must also block the wind, which otherwise swallows the body heat conserved by the first two layers. Other materials that approximate Gore-Tex and cost less are fine substitutes in cold dry climates.

Backcountry skiers should be

either your fleece layer or your Capilene layer. Some skiers wear nothing but a layer of underwear on warm days, but they carry extra layers.

Socks

Wool socks are as much a winter tradition as a warm fireplace. They are faithfully snug and keep frost from biting your toes. But against wool's rough surface, the ball and heel of your foot are like itchy blisters-in-waiting. A lightweight wool-polypro or Capilene-derivative undersock next to the feet is a blister-preventive layer that you won't notice unless you don't have it. Pull the wool sock on top and tuck your toes in for the ride.

Look for wool socks with smooth toe and heel seams; bulging seams can cause blisters or uncomfortable wrinkles. And bring an extra pair or two on multiday outings. In very cold weather, or if you are one of those unfortunates with perennially cold feet, use double boots that feature insulated inner booties.

Gaiters

If you plan to graduate to the backcountry, or even the odd trail-breaking outing through a local meadow, invest in a pair of gaiters. Without gaiters — or some type

Be sure to buy roomy, insulated gloves that won't reduce circulation to your fingers. For extreme cold, switch to mittens with liners.

Layering allows you to adjust clothing to your activity level. Having pitched camp, John Viehman and Terry Toyen will soon be reaching for their down coats to avoid becoming chilly.

of overboots — deep snow is radar-sharp at finding the bottom of your socks. In the backcountry, gaiters are as mandatory as skis. Made of sturdy, waterproof nylon blends, they fit over your boots and come up high enough to cover your calves. Find a pair with zippers that you can pull down if the day is especially warm or if the snow is only moderately deep.

Gloves

Remember two things about your hands. First, extremities are the

On blustery days, you'll be glad to have goggles, which protect eyes from snow glare, cold, wind, and windswept granules.

first to freeze, and second, activity stimulates circulation. Don't be surprised if shortly after you hit the snow, you find you need to reacquaint yourself with your fingertips, even if everything else is cozy. Yet after a few double-pole thrusts, you find your digits getting a second wind. Forcing the fingers to exercise will compel the circulatory system to route blood their way in order to energize them. Yes, poling makes the blood boil. Still, a multitiered layering system is as useful for your hands as it is for the

Designed by Bill Koch, World Cup and Olympic Nordic champion, this jacket, made of super-fine polypropylene, remains comfortable even during tough workouts.

rest of your body. And don't buy gloves that are too tight and cut off your circulation. Give your fingers at least enough space so the pumping blood can get to them.

Use a lightweight silk or nylon base layer underneath an insulating mitten. Even the bulkiest mitten should not encumber your poling ability, since you don't need to squeeze the poles hard — though inevitably, you will — in order to move them. If later on you feel you don't need the mittens, pocket them until the next time your fingers feel cold. Many skiers even strip off the base layer once they've truly warmed up. Base-layer gloves also allow you to keep your hands free enough to zip coats, strap bindings, and count your tumbles. Gotta love those one-hand days. Bring an extra pair of liners in case one is lost or gets wet.

Hats

Estimates vary as to just what percentage of heat is lost through your noggin. It's at least half, so when people tell you to keep a cool head, take them figuratively. If wool makes you do the monkey scratch, try a polypro-lined nylon alternative. Then if you overheat, bring an empty pocket in which to stuff your hat. Your head is your body's best thermostat, and removing a warm hat is the first thing you should do as you feel a sweat coming on as you herringbone up a long hill. Then, taking the reward of schussing down the other side, pull the hat back on as you feel a chill creep over you.

You'll learn to perform this hat trick without ever missing a stride. In very cold and/or windy conditions a balaclava — a mask-like hat that you pull on over your face, leaving only eyes and mouth exposed — may be the best choice.

Goggles

Since you're always in motion, it doesn't take a blizzard to impede your vision; a few flurries can do the trick. Especially on a blustery day, or in

When you're generating your own heat on the trail, outer layers soon come off altogether, and the zippers of pile jackets move down. If that's not enough, the wool hat will come off.

play. In the up-and-down terrain of the East, however, even well-adjusted goggles can get steamed up as you alternately sweat up a hill and cool off on the way down.

Sunglasses

Sun reflects like a spotlight off the snow. If you ski at altitude, don't underestimate the fact that there is more than a mile less atmosphere between you and the sun. Remember paper cuts? Eye burn is worse. Those who frequent the high country should look for sport-specific glasses that protect better against snow glare. Don't scrimp; purchase quality sunglasses.

Sunscreen

Sunburn is as bad as eye burn. Use a double-digit-numbered sunscreen (15 or higher), especially if you've been spending a lot of time behind a desk lately. Pay special attention to ears and nose. Also look out for the area under your chin, which is hardest hit by the reflection of the sun off the snow.

Lip Balm

Remember lip balm is not a treatment; it is a preventive. Ironically, the same folks who wouldn't dream of sun-worshiping without gobs of protection will wait to chap and peel before the first application of lip balm. Why? The stuff is cheap and portable, and it makes drinking from a cold glass a lot less excruciating.

any place where you aren't surrounded by trees that can intercept windswept granules, wearing goggles is prudent. Set the goggles comfortably so you don't have to adjust them midcourse; doing so will introduce moisture, and an internal fog is just as difficult to see through as a snow squall. Some goggles even come with interchangeable lenses for variable lighting and weather conditions. Goggles are a backcountry favorite, where longer downhill runs come into

WINTER SAFETY

One of cross-country skiing's most appealing elements is its low injury rate compared to other cardio-vascular activities. With proper precautions, cross-country is not dangerous sport. But if treated carelessly, the sport can become dangerous. Skiers should respect both the cold in which their activity takes place and, especially in the backcountry, the importance of maintaining manageable accessibility to shelter.

FROSTBITE

When blood fails to circulate properly to the extremities, exposed or poorly insulated skin tissue can easily freeze. The key word here is "circulation." Many skiers feel extreme cold in their hands at the beginning of a tour, but after five minutes of double-poling, their fingers are fine. The poling motion and the squeezing of the hands against the poles force blood to the arms, hands, and fingers, so circulation is not a problem. At the same time, the toes, perfectly toasty at the start of the tour, may be much colder, because they're scrunched inside a boot that is too tight.

In the early stages of frostbite, the skin is numb and lightly discolored. As the condition worsens, the color darkens and the skin hardens

and starts to shrivel. Don't wait for the early signs of frostbite to set in before doing something about it. Get inside as soon as possible. As long as you're outside, move your arms and fingers vigorously and wiggle your toes as best you can. You may even do well to remove gloves to blow on your hands and mime a few chords of air piano. You may do especially well to remove boots briefly if, in fact, boot tightness prevents you from wiggling your toes. If your socks are wet or simply aren't doing the job, stop and change them, wrapping something warm — perhaps another piece of clothing — around your bare feet and massaging vigorously to encourage circulation.

Treatment

Minor frostbite can be treated instantly by wrapping your extremities in warm clothing or placing them against body heat. Try tucking cold fingers inside your shirt and placing them against your stomach. But don't rub: even minor frostbite can lead to blisters that can pop and peel.

If skin has turned from pale white to gray to a shade of purple, severe frostbite has already set in, and your only priority should be to reach medical assistance as quickly as possible. Black skin will become paler at first, but will also end up purple when frostbitten. Do not attempt to thaw the affected area until you get inside for good or are certain that the area won't be

exposed to further cold. Thawing and refreezing is worse than leaving the frostbitten part alone until it can be warmed permanently. Once inside, treat minor frostbite by dunking fingers and toes in buckets of warm water and wiggling. Badly discolored skin should be treated immediately by a doctor.

In the case of ears and nose, try nudging tender parts of your face against your arms and shoulders. If your nose starts to run and you can't easily get to a tissue, blow hard through your nostrils and wipe your nose with your glove. It is best to avoid any moisture against your skin, even seemingly insignificant nose drips. This sounds unpleasant, but it is a sensible technique of frostbite prevention and well within the bounds of ski etiquette. Remember, nobody tells a marathon runner not to spit.

If you're in the backcountry, carry an emergency sleeping bag in your backpack. Sleeping bags may be bulky, but they aren't heavy. Most of your other survival items take up little space.

Carry chemical heat packs with you on any cross-country journey. They fit snugly into backpacks, even deep parka pockets, and are very effective at warding off frostbite.

Also, avoid touching or pressing your extremities against metal objects. You know the cruel school-yard trick of telling a younger child how much fun it is to touch your

Winter camping in the Logan Mountains, northern Utah. Always carry clothing for the coldest possible conditions for the season and location of your outing.

tongue to a lamppost or metal handrail.

HYPOTHERMIA

The dictionary calls it "subnormal temperature of the body." Basically, it's the cooling of your insides and the consequent slowing of your metabolic processes. It can occur in surprisingly warm temperatures (25 to 50°F). Cross-country skiers are especially in danger of becoming hypothermic when they stop skiing, radically reducing their expenditure of energy. Cross-country skiing generates plenty of body heat, so it's easy to forget just how cold it is until you stop exercising. When you do, pull on a hat and another layer of clothing (see Chapter 8) before you start to shiver. Warning signs of hypothermia include uncontrollable shivering followed by dizziness, slurred speech, disorientation, and pulse reduction. In the stages leading up to hypothermia, it is very easy to reverse the trend.

Antidotes include warm liquids, quick carbos, and a change into dry clothes. Avoid alcohol. It pulls heat out of the body and increases hypothermia's severity. Hot chocolate will hit the spot, but avoid drinks containing caffeine. Bring along a candy bar or a pack of raisins or trail mix to fill your body's fuel tank. A warm blanket and your favorite wool sweater, a bad idea for active touring, will snuggle you just fine once you get indoors.

Don't take hypothermia lightly. If

The keys to preventing altitude sickness are ascending the heights gradually to allow your body to adjust and drinking plenty of fluids.

you work up too much body heat in too short a period of time, you will cause your body to soak in cold sweat, magnifying the cold conditions outside. Don't venture too far away from shelter unless you know the weather forecast. Conditions, especially mountain conditions, can change quickly, and what seemed manageable 10 minutes earlier may suddenly be turning into a problem if you're not prepared. As the body temperature drops, the domino effect of fluid loss, pulse reduction, and equilibrium loss can be sudden. At and below 92°F, the body is no longer able to warm itself without outside help. Again, if you fail to take steps, the process will accelerate.

Oddly enough, body-to-body heat, a once-prescribed, seemingly logical solution to hypothermia, may actually cause more harm than good. A hypothermic person will collect acidic blood in the muscles. If the blood is warmed too quickly, this toxic blood rushes back to the heart, where it can cause cardiac arrest. If a heat pack is available, place it in the underarm or groin area of the patient to allow the blood circulating in major vessels to warm up. If a person becomes hypothermic, be sure to get him dry and sheltered from the elements as fast as possible. Do not let him have alcohol, fall asleep, or continue his physical exertion even if he says he feels fine. And have a member of your party seek medical help immediately.

ALTITUDE SICKNESS

For many skiers in the western United States, a cross-country journey is a foray into unknown heights. Skiers who already live at altitude may have little trouble with an ascent into the mountains. But if you're a sea-level dweller who is spending a vacation on skis, with an ascent of several thousand feet comes a dizzying boulder-on-the-shoulder queasiness that saps your wind, your energy, and even your appetite.

with water and leaving the bathroom door open during the night. The water will evaporate gradually, acting as a humidifier and compensating for the dry air you've been breathing outside. You could also simply carry a portable humidifier with you if you have a rental car or place you can store it.

Serious injury among cross-country skiers is rare, but accidents do occur, especially during races. Immediate, trained attention is vital on frigid days.

Prevention

Common sense tells you to avoid alcohol and drink water. Even if you don't feel thirsty, make sure to stay hydrated. Include soups with meals, when possible, and avoid foods with a creamy consistency. If you are urinating only twice a day, you're not drinking enough water. If your urine is bright yellow, you are not drinking enough; if it is clear, you're all right. Take water with you everywhere you go. A water bottle should be as essential to your Nordic adventure as a pair of skis.

If you're staying in a hotel or inn along the way, try filling your bathtub

Medications

Advil or Tylenol should fight your headache, but Diamox, the best-known prescription preventive for altitude sickness, must be taken 48 hours prior to ascent in order to be effective. It is not a cure.

ACUTE MOUNTAIN SICKNESS

AMS usually strikes within 12 hours of ascent. It is caused by a decreased concentration of oxygen in the blood

and can leave you nauseous, tired, dizzy, and winded. If you have a Rocky Mountain ski weekend planned, you'll probably recover from AMS just in time for your return to sea level.

To avoid AMS, stagger your ascent over more than one day. Take several days if possible. Don't climb more than 2,000 to 3,000 feet in a day if you can fit it into your schedule. Once you reach the back-country, cut the rate of ascent down to 1,000 feet per day. The higher you go, the more you'll need to slow your ascent. Climb gradually, avoiding ski lifts and snowmobiles. One good itinerary for those heading into the Rocky Mountains might be: On day one, fly to Denver, at 5,000 feet; on day two, drive halfway to Boulder, at 8,000 feet; on day three, complete the drive; on day four, ski up to a novice trail or hut system at 9,000 feet; on day five, ski up to a more advanced hut at 9,750 feet; and so on.

Without complications, AMS is never fatal and usually does no more than ruin your ski weekend, but it can lay the foundations for more severe ailments. It is much better to prevent it than to cure it after the fact.

High-Altitude Pulmonary Edema

Think of high-altitude pulmonary edema (HAPE) as acute mountain sickness accompanied by a nasty cough. This may not seem like much of an additional burden, but the cough can lead to pneumonia and fluid buildup in the lungs and can also be a sign of critical oxygen loss that can be fatal within days if you're as high as 14,000 feet.

Beginning American back-country skiers probably won't climb that high unless they leave their country and their senses behind. Still, if the frog jumps into your throat, it's time to descend or seek help.

FIRST AID KITS

Basic first aid kits should address both minor problems such as cuts and blisters and certain emergencies. You may also want to stash extra food rations with your first aid kit to better organize your space.

Keep separate kits or separate compartments within kits for first aid and gear-repair paraphernalia. Items that overlap (e.g., tweezers and scissors) should be placed in the first aid kit. Be sure to position the first aid kit in your pack so that it is easy to reach in an emergency. With luck you won't need it.

The sample first aid kit (see sidebar) is incomplete but also includes items you'll probably ignore. Just as you would when you pack for an extended vacation, it's best to prepare a list long before your departure so you can add to it as things come to mind. Simply check them off as you build your stash: aspirin, Band-Aids,

Contents of a Sample First Aid Kit

For the backcountry skier, as for the backpacker, the contents of a first aid kit must balance need against weight. For many, purchasing a ready-made kit is the simplest way to include the necessities. Others prefer to customize their kits, and so make a trip to the drugstore armed with a carefully prepared list. Here is one such list — slightly modified for use on winter trips — prepared by Karen Berger, distance backpacker and author of the Trailside Guide *Hiking & Backpacking*.

- Names and numbers of people to contact in an emergency
- Blister kit (including Second Skin, 1-inch-wide medicine tape, moleskin, and a needle)
- Antibiotic ointment (Neosporin or Bacitracin)
- Hydrogen peroxide or rubbing alcohol for disinfecting (a 2- or 3-ounce plastic bottle is plenty)
- Painkillers
- Rubber gloves
- Medicine tape (1 inch wide — doubles for repair on gear)
- Tweezers and scissors (your army knife may have them)
- Ace bandage
- Gauze (2-inch roll)
- Gauze pads (several 3-inch and 4-inch squares
- Band-Aids and butterfly closures
- Medicines: cold tablets, antihistamines, throat lozenges, Alka-Seltzer; if you're going on an extended trip, ask your doctor about prescribing a general antibiotic
- Personal prescription drugs, including drugs for bee stings, if you are allergic
- Extra moleskin
- Antidiarrheal
- Tincture of benzoin

A probe pole can be useful in pinpointing the location of an avalanche victim, but it is no substitute for a transceiver.

Causes

Sudden changes in weather create conditions conducive to snow sliding, one reason you should always check weather forecasts before any backcountry journey. As a rule, the less time it takes a snowpack to accumulate, the more volatile the pack is likely to be. Additionally, a foot of wet, heavy snow will slide more easily than a foot of lighter powder. Recent rainfall will change the composition of crystals. Heavy or even moderate winds can change the angle of the crystals and increase the likelihood of collapse.

Trees are generally effective windbreaks and snow holders. If you pass through a crowded forest into an area unguarded by vegetation, put yourself on avalanche alert. The lack of trees could indicate past avalanche activity. Also, be aware that avalanches generally strike the same

gauze pads, Ace bandages, bandage adhesive, tissues, heat packs, vitamins, medicines, tweezers, scissors, blister kit (including moleskin).

AVALANCHES

Humans provide the trigger for the majority of avalanches. The seemingly insignificant weight of one passing skier can unsettle a snowpack and engulf the trespasser. Each year, 20 people die in avalanche accidents throughout the mountainous regions of the United States. Skiers of all levels who enter avalanche zones should respect the power of avalanches and seek out instruction in recognizing avalanche risk and preventing and avoiding avalanches.

However transfixing the beauty of the high country in winter, travelers there must be mindful of avalanche zones. An experienced guide is the best insurance against crossing avalanche-prone slopes.

place more than once. Ask your local forest service if your route has any history of avalanches.

Avoiding and Surviving Avalanches

Once you are able to recognize avalanche zones, your first priority is to do everything in your power to go

slope is angled between 30 and 50 degrees, you should find a way to ski above the avalanche zone, on a route with less severe slope. Skiing below it may keep you from starting an avalanche, but will do nothing to keep you from getting caught in one if it starts. And if some of the conditions mentioned above are present — e.g., heavy winds, recent precipitation, heavy snow — you may want to avoid open slopes as gentle as 25 degrees.

TESTING THE SNOW. You can test the snowpack by jabbing the snow with your pole. Poke through as far as your pole will reach, feeling for any soft layers. If

John Viehman and Steve Howe use transceivers to locate avalanche victims quickly enough to dig them out before they run short on oxygen. Carry a lightweight, retractable shovel for digging.

around them. If circumvention isn't practical, you should know how to cross these zones in relative safety. As an emergency precaution, you should know what to do if you or someone traveling with you is stuck in the middle of one.

SLOPE METER. If you come upon terrain that looks like an avalanche zone, you can use a slope meter to tell you the angle of the slope you're thinking of crossing. Generally if a

the pack seems firm and consistent, you are in good shape. If the layers are distinguishable as you poke through, this may indicate that a flimsy layer could slide on a firm layer if given the impetus to move. These "slab avalanches" are the most dangerous, because huge slabs of snow can move, breaking up as they build speed.

CROSSING. If you must cross an open area, do it safely. Make sure only one

member of your group crosses at a time. If that member encounters trouble, the others can help him or her. If you plan to travel alone, the advice is simple: Stay away from avalanche zones at all times.

Before you cross, make sure your clothing articles are buttoned and fastened. If your backpack attaches at the waist, make sure to unfasten the waist buckle in case you get caught and need to fling off the pack. Slip your wrists out of your pole straps, since you'll want your hands free during an avalanche. If you notice skittish snow in the beginning of your crossing, retrace your steps and search for a more secure crossing. Angle your skis slightly downslope as you cross.

IF YOU'RE CAUGHT. If you sense that an avalanche is just forming, try to ski to the edge of the falling pack. Once the falling snow makes skiing impossible, jettison your poles and pack and start waving your arms as though you were swimming the backstroke. This may enable you to stay above the snow or at least close to the surface. If your arms are no longer able to swing, place your hands over your nose and mouth to form a breathing pocket. You probably won't have time to unlatch your

Lightweight (9.8 oz), battery-operated avalanche beacons can save lives. They should be worn by every member of a ski party traveling in avalanche country.

skis, but do it if you can.

AVALANCHE BEACONS. These transceivers can run as high as $300, but if you ever need one, no price is too high. All members of your party should wear one under their clothing and leave them tuned to the "transmit" mode while they tour. If you plan to cross first, leave your beacon on "transmit," but have your partners set theirs to "receive." If you encounter trouble, the transmission will alert them to your location. Make sure all your transceivers have compatible frequencies. Beacons are slowly being standardized, but some transceivers will not pick up certain transmissions. If you plan to purchase beacons before traveling with a particular group, make sure you're all on the same frequency. Then test your beacons before and during travel, and take extra batteries along just in case.

SHOVEL. Using only your ski poles to extricate an engulfed friend on short oxygen supply can be like looking for a needle in a haystack with another needle. You probably have no more than five or ten minutes to free someone from an avalanche. Poles

Approach snow bridges cautiously, testing their strength as you proceed. A drenching in winter far from shelter is a serious matter.

Find out if your route has any established water hazards, such as small lakes and streams, that you'll need to cross. All should have secure bridges or be shallow enough so that you can stand on the bottom with your head above water. Never cross anything that appears deep enough to cover your head. If you're not sure, take a pass. Similarly, if you reach a patch of what looks like thin ice, don't take chances. Ski around it. But in case you do get caught, as always, be prepared.

The more easily you are able to free yourself from the confines of your ski gear, the more easily you'll be able to swim or otherwise navigate your way to safety. Allow yourself to carry whatever you are able to hoist at your side. Get out of your ski poles and carry them, so you can free your hands. If you can do the same with your skis, your backpack, anything that will increase your range of movement ahead of time, do it.

Getting Wet

If you fall into the drink, drop all of your gear and get out as soon as possible. Saving your equipment is not as important as getting dried off and preventing hypothermia, even if the water doesn't reach your waist. Assuming you're able to stand up in the water, remove your skis and walk across until you reach firm ground. Stay unencumbered so that you can swim if, as you walk across, the water

and skis are not meant for digging; you need a shovel. Look for a firm, molded-plastic, retractable model that fits onto your backpack. The blade should have reasonably sharp edges that can pierce through snow, yet still be firm enough to remove the snow once you start pulling. Only extend the shovel far enough so that it transfers your force quickly through the snowpack.

PROBE POLE. Most backcountry ski poles come with detachable baskets and handles that allow you to connect two poles lengthwise to make one long pole. Still, poles are a poor locating substitute for beacons and a poor digging substitute for shovels.

becomes too deep. Keep calm and find a piece of equipment or patch of thick ice that can help you float. If you're traveling with companions, have them connect their poles so you have something to grab onto.

Drying Off

Replace all wet clothing with dry clothes as soon as possible. If this means exposing bare skin to the elements while you change, do it. Those few moments of exposure are better than waiting for wet clothes to dry while they refrigerate you. If, after changing all you're able to change, you still have wet gear pressing against you, take the most direct route to the indoors.

NAVIGATION

Weather Forecasts

Beware of impending storms and other climatic changes that could affect your journey. If you plan to be away for, say, five days, be sure to pack for the full range of weather that might occur. Don't just walk outside and say, "Hmm, this jacket feels okay." If you hear of an approaching frontal system and know that the temperature is near the freezing point, be ready to tackle ice, deep snow, hardpack, and slush at some point during your trip. The better prepared you are, the less you'll worry.

Trail Markers

NORDIC CENTERS. Most centers use the following symbols to classify course difficulty: green circles for beginners, blue squares for intermediates, black diamonds for advanced. That isn't the case everywhere, so ask the center's personnel which markings it uses. The easier courses have more gradual turns and less severe gradients. Markings should appear at least every mile or kilometer and be marked accordingly by their distance from the entrance to the center. But again, standards differ from place to place.

At centers where skating is permitted only on certain trails, look for icons of skaters with or without an "X" through the icon telling you whether skating is or isn't permitted on that particular trail.

An exclamation point surrounded by a red diamond is a sign for some type of caution. Heed it and ski somewhere else, or at least proceed with caution.

BACKCOUNTRY. Tourers should ask experienced locals about the clarity, nature, and frequency of markings on their proposed route. The standards vary more when you leave the Nordic center, so be sure to know what you're looking for. Recent storms and windswept snow can erase established tracks that make it easy to follow routes. Wind-driven snow can also obscure trail markers. The blazes on Vermont's Long Trail, for example, are white, and so are difficult to find in winter. If you miss one marking and can't retrace your steps,

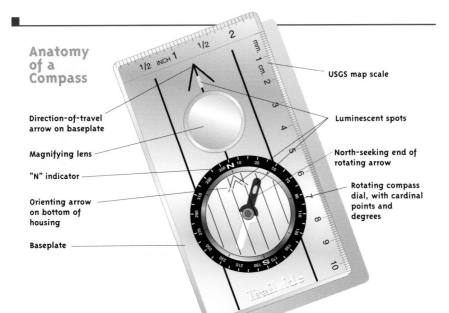

Anatomy of a Compass

Direction-of-travel arrow on baseplate

Magnifying lens

"N" indicator

Orienting arrow on bottom of housing

Baseplate

USGS map scale

Luminescent spots

North-seeking end of rotating arrow

Rotating compass dial, with cardinal points and degrees

you must be able to find your way without them. Be sure to buy the most complete guidebooks to the backcountry you intend to tour, and study the guides and topographic maps closely in advance of your trip.

Orienteering with Map and Compass

Everyone in your group should have basic orienteering skills, and at least one person should be intimately familiar with the area you're entering. A course of map and compass instruction is recommended for novices, even if their companions are experienced. There is no way to know if you will be comfortable using a map and compass together until you try it. Take some sort of instruction and then go into the woods with an accomplished orienteerer who can show the details to you firsthand.

MAPS. Most landmarks, trails, and even roads will be listed in some sort of guidebook. Maps may be included with guidebooks or pamphlets pertaining to a particular area. But once you start breaking your own trail, extending either the length or complexity of your journey, you are more likely to need topographic maps. Depending on the scale of the map, the information may be very detailed or relatively undetailed.

Learn how particular features such as rivers, lakes, and ridges are shown on maps. Green shading indicates that an area is wooded. Absence of shading generally indicates open spaces that may be great for Telemarking and parallel skiing, but may also be avalanche zones if the slope is severe, as indicated by the spacing of contour lines on the

Taking a Bearing

Start by pointing the directional arrow of your compass at a prominent tree, hilltop, or other landmark whose bearing you want to know. Now rotate the compass dial so that the needle and the "N" indicator are aligned. Next, adjust for declination. The "N" indicator is now pointing to true north; the needle continues to point to magnetic north; and the directional arrow tells you the bearing of your landmark.

map. Tight contour lines indicate steep terrain that may include avalanche areas and cliffs; widely spaced lines indicate gentler terrain.

Always check the year your topo map was made, since the landscape changes over time. Alterations, both natural and man-made, can create or eliminate roads, lakes, and large sec-

tions of vegetation. And be aware that a map can only tell you so much. No map can tell you how difficult it will be to find certain landmarks in dense fog.
COMPASSES AND FINDING NORTH. Your compass is like a spare set of eyes that can see what yours can't. A compass allows you to quantify your

directions to places you can see, follow directional bearings to places you can't see, and identify both landmarks and your proximity to them. There are no street signs in the backcountry, and in a pinch, a compass becomes your lifeline.

All landmark sightings require you to find north. Unfortunately, the needle in a compass points not to true north, but rather to magnetic north, a spot whose exact bearing relative to that of the actual North Pole changes from year to year. For the most part, the differential between the two norths depends on where you are. This adds an additional necessary step to compass use.

If you're touring in New England, your needle will point slightly west of true north. If you're touring in the Rockies, it will point slightly east of true north. Topographic maps distinguish between the two by including a star-topped arrow that points to true north and another arrow that points to magnetic north — it should be marked "MN." These arrows show the difference in degrees between true and magnetic north for any given topo map. You will need to account for the difference, known as the declination, when you use your compass and map together to make proper alignments. It may sound simple, but remember to distinguish between the arrow, which you control, and the needle, controlled by Mother Nature.

Here's another reason to use current maps. The declination of a particular region should be listed on the map's lower left corner. The newer the map, the less likely you are to misalign your arrow based on an outdated magnetic north reading. Take the adjustable arrow on your compass and move it X number of degrees east or west on the MN needle based on the declination listed on your map. Now your arrow is pointing to true north.

MAP AND COMPASS TOGETHER. Lay the map flat, place the compass on it, and orient the compass to true north. Now rotate the map under the compass so that the legend that shows true north is lined up with true north on your compass. When you have done this, the map, the compass, and the terrain will all be aligned with each other.

If you know where you are and you want to identify a landmark, take a compass bearing of the landmark. Now the directional arrow is pointing not north, but to the landmark. Put the compass back down on the map, making sure that the line of the directional arrow runs through your current position on the map. The arrow is pointing toward the landmark.

TRIANGULATING. Remember the right angles and triangles you created in geometry class, wondering if you would ever use them in real life? It's time. If you don't know where you are or are uncertain of your location, triangulating will pinpoint your position.

Arrange the map and compass so that they are aligned with the terrain as above. Now, take an educated guess as to where you are by carefully observing the surrounding landscape and matching it to the terrain represented on the topo map. Look for distinctive features like ledges, prominent peaks, deep ravines. Now take a bearing of one such landmark and place the compass on the map as above, pointing the directional arrow to the landmark. Draw a line representing that arrow. Then take a bearing of a second landmark, preferably at right angles to the first landmark. The lines on the map that you've just drawn will intersect at the

A CAUTIONARY WINTER'S TALE

In February 1993, a group of seven skiers headed out toward a hut in the Elk Mountains of Colorado's backcountry. Their experience level varied; two skiers had many hours on snow but were headed for a hut for the first time, two men had climbed the Himalayan mountains and knew the backcountry as intimately as their backyard, and the rest were in between. Forecasts suggested rough weather, but the group forged on, confident that their collective smarts and experience would keep them safe.

The next day, hemmed in by blizzard conditions, they crossed a path with no trees or trail markings. Realizing that the group was lost, the two most experienced skiers told the others to wait while they skied for help. "If we're not back in half an hour," the men said, "follow us in the same direction." The group's members had just committed the first cardinal sin of getting lost: they split up.

After half an hour, the two group leaders had changed course, making their steps impossible to follow because of their poor directions and the windswept tracks underfoot. Eventually, the two men reached a phone after spending many hours in the woods.

The other five members soon split up. The least-experienced pair attempted to retrace their steps. Through trial, error, and instinct, they reached their cars successfully and survived. The other three found a cabin and were eventually rescued after fighting over use of two sleeping bags. Still, five days in the wilderness had taken their toll on one woman, who suffered severe frostbite to her fingers and had part of a thumb removed in a Denver hospital.

that allow you to ski on and find the hut, road, river, mountaintop, or parking lot you're trying to reach.

GROUP TRAVEL

The three most important rules of group travel are easy to remember: Stay together, stay together, and stay together.

A pair of seasoned mountain men may be fine together in the woods, but if your group includes even one inexperienced back-

Do not venture out into the backcountry in a group of fewer than four. If a mishap occurs, stay together. Splitting up usually leads to even more serious consequences.

spot where you're standing. If you want to be certain, take three bearings. There may be a slight variation of intersection points, but no matter how many bearings you take, you should still end up in the same place.

Once you know your own location, you can keep taking bearings

country skier, a team of anywhere from four to eight skiers is probably most advisable.

Prudent Formation

As you ski, have the group's slowest, least experienced member close to the front. He shouldn't lead, of

course, but he shouldn't bring up the rear, either, since if he does, it will be easier to lose him. If the terrain is wide enough, put the slowest member beside a "group leader" — group leaders should be the most experienced skiers or the ones most familiar with the area, not necessarily the fastest — and have the slow skier set the pace for the group. Keep an experienced skier at the group's anchor so that the trailers don't become stragglers who could eventually lose contact with the others. Keep the distance between skiers to a minimum. Better skiers can simply make conversation to keep the trailers amused. If the group is large, take periodic headcounts. Do this during water breaks, which should be frequent anyway. Never hesitate to ask your group to slow down or stop so you can rehydrate.

Getting Lost

If you lose your way, don't panic. Stay together! Under certain conditions, you may be better off staying put than wandering aimlessly and taking a chance that you will get yourself lost even more. If it becomes clear that your group doesn't know the direction of its destination, your next option is to try retracing your steps. It is usually unwise to move in heavy snowfall or darkness, though a full moon is usually a better guidelight than you might think, and dangerous nearby conditions may force you to move. As you proceed, keep thinking

of places to build emergency shelter if you feel you should park for the night or simply find a way to warm up.

EMERGENCY SHELTER

Don't be alarmed. This is a bit like knowing which exit to use in case of a fire: you should never need to employ the directions, but you should always know how to follow them. If you take proper precautions, a planned day trip should never turn into an overnight stay. But you should know how to take care of yourself if it does and you don't have a sleeping bag or a place to go.

Construction

You'll need to dig a snow cave from a firm mound, preferably in an area next to a wind-breaking tree. If it's well constructed, a snow cave can keep you quite warm. Remember, Eskimos have used them for centuries. First either find a snowdrift or begin piling snow to create a packed mound that ideally reaches to roughly your height.

Once you have a mound, begin at the base and start digging horizontally. Ideally using a shovel, but more likely your ski poles, remove snow and gradually create a dome-shaped cavity inside the snowbank. The ceiling should be at least 18 inches thick. Pat the inside walls with your hands or gloves, creating a somewhat liquefied inner coating that prevents the ceiling from caving in. Detach

your ski pole handles and poke a few holes in the ceiling to permit air circulation. The snow should be packed tightly enough so the ceiling won't start to tumble. Don't use a bank that is too high. If it does collapse while you're asleep, you need to worm your way out. Also, since warm air rises, try to keep the entrance as low as possible, with an inner platform for sleeping. That way the colder air can work its way out of the cave and be replaced by warmer air.

Make some sort of bed for yourself inside the cave. Use your backpack, an extra jacket, even tree branches to keep your body away from the snow while you sleep.

THE FITNESS FACTOR

Cross-country skiing will engage every part of the body and provide a superb means of maintaining or increasing general fitness that complements virtually any other physical activity. Apart from the sport's inherently pristine air and stress-melting surroundings, cross-country strengthens the heart, lungs, and muscles without extracting a pounding fee from impact-sensitive joints.

Those who catch the cross-country bug may want some related off-season activities to keep them in shape for ski season. And just as skiers can use other sports as cross-training activities, athletes who regu-

larly engage in other sports can use cross-country skiing to build a fitness base that will help them with their primary activities.

CROSS-COUNTRY SKIING AS A CROSS-TRAINER

While much of this book may suit the part-time or infrequent athlete, those who use cross-country skiing for cross-training purposes are only going to do so if they are very competent in another sport. You don't have to be a world-class athlete to fit into that category, but here are the stories of a few who are or were, and the ways in which they have bene-

fited from skiing cross-country. They are a testament to cross-country skiing's place in the very first rank of sports that provide overall muscular and aerobic fitness.

RUNNING
Grete Waitz

The legendary Norwegian won one Olympic silver medal and nine New York City Marathons, but Waitz's introduction to competition took place on snow, stumbling as she tried to keep up with classmates or kick a ball that was embedded in the snow. "That is how we played when we were younger," Waitz says. "The games we would play on skis formed our sense of balance, we spent so many hours playing."

DID YOU KNOW

While skiing amongst Manchurian frost, Norwegian missionaries even tried spreading their word of the Cross and the gospel of cross-country during winters in Northern China. Then they pushed on to Japan. Judging from today's abundant following of bicycling and Buddhism, their conversion rate was probably low on both fronts.

Waitz never lost the cultural connection to her childhood and used many opportunities to replace roads with trails. "When your mileage is 100-plus miles a week, some of those miles are not that tough," she says. "Sometimes I was just about jogging. When I reached that point, I did some of the miles on skis and enjoyed them more. If the roads were bad, I would substitute [skiing for] three or four runs."

Waitz also found cross-country to be easier on her ankles than roadwork. "It was one of the things that saved my legs all those years," she says. In the mid-1980s, Grete suffered a stress fracture and was unable to run at all during the summer. She experimented with a NordicTrack machine, simulating her running intervals or keeping a steady pace for up to an hour. "It was effective," she says, "but tough mentally, very boring. You don't get to see any mountains on a NordicTrack."

Both Waitz and longtime Norwegian rival Ingrid Kristiansen split their time between the United States and Norway and introduced many fellow runners to Nordic skiing. For elite runners, Waitz points out, it takes sufficient aptitude on skis to get the type of cardiovascular workout they're accustomed to

United States team member Ben Husaby in the cross-country relay, Les Saisies, France. World-class athletes in many sports attest to the superb all-round conditioning cross-country provides.

getting from running. "People who use bad technique will get a bad workout," she says. "If you're not stable on your skis, then you don't get any benefit from it. Once you know what you're doing, no type of cross-training compares to it."

Bob Kempainen

The 1992 Olympian grew up learning how to ski cross-country in his native Minnetonka, Minnesota. "A lot of elite runners in the state found it more enjoyable than trying to battle the winter elements," recalls Kempainen, whose brother Todd was an alternate on the 1980 Olympic cross-country team. "Whenever runners could find an excuse to put on the

?

DID YOU KNOW

Twelve years after sweeping three individual events at the Sarajevo Games, Finland's Maria-Liisa Kirvesneimi upped her medal total to seven by capturing two bronzes in 1994, at age 38. When she still went by her maiden name, Maria-Liisa Hamalainen was said to have illegally oxygenated her blood, a pharmaceutical no-no that gave rise to the sardonic whisper Maria-Liisa Hemoglobin.

skis, they usually did."

What's more, they also avoided the perils of winter footing, which had the effect of frozen granite on one step and banana peels on the next. "If you're somebody with a history of injury, to go four months through the winter is not a good idea," Kempainen says. "Maybe a few miles a couple of times is OK, but if you're just going to limp along anyway worrying about your footing, you'd be better off skiing once a day for 20 kilometers. You'll get a better workout and you won't aggravate the injury."

No longer a competitive skier, Kempainen often alternated first and second place with a fellow runner/skier named Ben Husaby in the state cross-country championships. Husaby was also junior national champion in cross-country running.

"Every year after I'd been skiing, I'd come into the spring with so much strength work, I'd usually be ahead of the game by May. But the great thing is I wouldn't get tired the way I think you would if you put in all those hours on the roads."

OAR AND PADDLE SPORTS

Perhaps only swimmers tax their arms with the rhythmic tempo of cross-country skiers the way athletes with paddles and oars do. Even Ping-Pong players take a break between points.

Flat-water kayak racers and tourers are among the few athletes who relentlessly tax (and condition) their shoulders and arms the way cross-country skiers do.

Hartmut Buschbacker (rowing)

Before he became coach of the U.S. Women's Rowing Team, Buschbacker spent four years on the national team in East Germany, where the government-run sports industry faced no budgetary restraints in developing and practicing the latest high-tech training methods. Olympians did not spend their spare time at the bowling alley, and their cross-training always received the stamp of officialdom.

Throughout his career, Buschbacker practiced cross-country skiing as a staple of his preparation for international competition. From January through March, he and his teammates trained twice a day for between two and six hours on various trails throughout Europe, even though the team's immense budget allowed the rowers to travel to warm-weather sites for year-round paddling. "It's the best type of training for the end of a [rowing] race," Buschbacker explains. "One thing with cross-country: when you accelerate, you can maintain that acceleration longer. Your muscles, I think, stay closer to the edge of burn without burning better than they do in any other sport. The first time in the spring when I would do some rowing, I felt in the last hundred meters or so that the training base of

cross-country was helping me. Maybe in my mind I was thinking, 'I'm not really burning,' you know.

"It is a great all-body sport, but it has a different approach to balance. In rowing, the water is always flat; in cross-country, you are going uphill and then downhill. Also in rowing you are not shifting weight so

> 66 If you cross-country ski three times a week, you never have to do anything else. You never have to go to a gym. It works all the muscles in your body. Cross-country skiing is an overall fitness sport. 99
>
> — Greg Lemond,
> three-time winner of the
> Tour de France
> and the United State's
> most decorated cyclist

much. Always you are traveling straight with equal emphasis on the right side and left side. I think cross-country helped not with the mechanics of balance, but maybe with the discipline of keeping some kind of balance pattern, which you must do in rowing. For any sport that does not permit a stop, this [cross-country] is a good mirror."

Buschbacker sees a day when U.S. rowers will incorporate Nordic skiing into off-season preparation. "Because of maybe geography and sporting culture, Americans are not so exposed to it. But at the beginning levels and elite levels, there is great benefit."

Unlike most aerobic athletes, canoeists and kayakers practice sports that emphasize the arms and often use cross-country skiing to help their legs the way a runner would to add strength to the arms. Rowers expand and contract their legs with every stroke of the oars, but canoeists and kayakers have their legs wedged into their vehicles as if they were in straitjackets.

Chuck Lyda
(canoeing and kayaking)

An Olympian in both canoeing (1976) and kayaking (1980), Lyda was also a world champion in the non-Olympic sport of white-water canoe slalom in 1975 and 1977. A southern California native, Lyda had never been on cross-country skis before moving to the Olympic Training Center in Squaw Valley, California, at age 24. There, at the site of the 1960 Winter Olympics, Lyda quickly took to Nordic skiing for purely cross-training purposes. "I wasn't really doing a leg sport," Lyda recalls. "But in the canoe all that upper-body power still has to be supported through the legs. Skiing worked the whole package better than anything."

Lyda, at first only a diagonal

"The double-poling motion in cross-country is similar to what you do in the canoe," says canoe and kayak medalist Chuck Lyda.

strider, was tempted to over-pole and would fudge his steps rather than stretch his legs through the glide. "Technique was a problem," Lyda admits, even though he had also been a competitive cyclist as a teenager. Still, he adapted and became proficient enough on the trails to make the U.S. national team in biathlon four times.

"The double-poling motion in cross-country is similar to what you do in the canoe," he says. "The top arm drives down hard, and at the bottom you have to roll back. Kayaking involves a straight pull back after the paddle is rotated out.

"Your oblique muscles — your abdominals and laterals — gain strength through skiing cross-country, which also strengthens your lower back. Most people who do paddle sports don't work the antagonistic muscles enough in their cross-training. They go to the gym, get bulky, help their arms, do a little for their legs. but ignore their lower back. Then once the season starts they get injured. Cross-country is such a complete workout, it also prevents injury by not allowing you to overlook anything."

Unlike most canoeists and kayakers, who would gain weight after reducing their cardiovascular output during the winter, Lyda found that he arrived for the spring's training season lighter, fitter, and, best of all, able to eat with abandon. "Everyone hated me for that," he recalls.

Robert Gaggoli tries to jump away from the pack. Many cyclists find that cross-country is the off-season sport that gives them the maximum workout they need to stay in shape.

In December 1984, Lyda and his fellow biathletes were stunned to find their European foes employing the skating technique when the Americans arrived for their first World Cup race of the season in An Thlotz, Italy. "Everybody just skated by us," Lyda remembers. "We were caught with our pants down."

But Lyda found the technique more to his liking than his U.S. teammates did, since his familiarity with canoeing's twisting motion enabled him to adapt to the emphasis on weight transfer and more powerful upper-body phase of skating. During the season, Lyda's U.S. ranking jumped from sixth to third, an improvement he attributes to his successful adjustment to skating.

Unlike Buschbacker, Lyda ultimately preferred skating to the diagonal stride. "Rowers have more of a linear motion to their stroke than we do," he says. "A rower might prefer the classical techniques; a canoe-kayaker, I think, could benefit more from skating. It can take 10 years to become a good diagonal strider. Skaters can pick it up much quicker."

CYCLING
Davis Phinney

The Colorado native competed frequently in cross-country citizen races as a teenager, but at 18, he opted for cycling as his primary sport. During the early years of his career on

wheels, Phinney stayed away from the trails and captured a bronze medal in the cycling team trial at the 1984 Los Angeles Olympics.

But Phinney confessed that he could never shake "this thing that was in me about loving winter and snow. I had denied it for 10 years, but it was always there."

He reintroduced Nordic skiing into his training regimen and became so hooked that he and fellow riders Greg Lemond, Tom Schuler, Mike King, and Jeff Bradley started the Great Lakes Ski Team in 1990. Soon the cyclists were all entering cross-country races during the winter months that had effectively been down-cycles in their training. While most of his fellow cyclists opted for skating, Phinney found that he still preferred the familiar classical strides.

"I loved it because it brought the same glutes and quads into play that I used in cycling," Phinney says. "Of course, I went out every day for two or three months. But if you have the capability, two to four days of cross-country per week is a good cross-trainer for almost any endurance-based sport.

"The mistake most cyclists made is that they found it very hard to get the maximum workout. Cross-country uses all the muscles at the same time, and if you don't have the fundamentals of technique it's like you're fighting yourself if you're trying to get in a really good workout. It's great if you ski efficiently, but not if you just slog around.

"Also some guys forgot they weren't on bikes anymore. They fig-

SURVIVAL OF THE CROSS-COUNTRY SKIERS

In one seven-year stretch, athletes with a background in cross-country skiing won the made-for-television event known as the "Survival of the Fittest" on six occasions. The event included athletes from a dozen different primary sports. "I'm not sure what that proves," confesses Lyle Nelson, a 13-year veteran of the U.S. biathlon team and "Survival"

champion in 1984. "But I guess it says if you have a cross-country base, you can pick up other sports pretty quick."

The "Survival" event incorporated cross-country running, kayaking, mountain biking, and mountain climbing. "If you look at the full range of ways in which those other sports test your ability, cross-country skiing, including backcountry skiing, does all the same things," says Nelson.

never have to do anything else," Lemond says. "You never have to go to a gym. It works all the muscles in your body. Cross-country skiing is an overall fitness sport. The competition is great, a lot like cycling in that you always have to push it."

Roller skiing is one of the preferred ways for cross-country athletes to remain fully conditioned during off-season months. In-line skating, they find, is not satisfactory. A pair of roller skis (opposite) cost about $250.

ured they'd have to be out there for five or six hours. That's fine for back-country touring. But all you really need is one or two hours."

Phinney, who retired from competition in 1993, also found that he and his fellow cyclists enjoyed "not having to dodge in and out of traffic all the time the way you do on the roads. You can't explain the difference in stress between fighting traffic and just enjoying the fluidity and scenery of cross-country. Once you understand it, you get the bug and it stays with you."

The bug also caught Lemond, a three-time winner of the Tour de France and the most decorated U.S. cyclist in history. "If you cross-country ski three times a week, you

CROSS-TRAINING FOR CROSS-COUNTRY SKIERS

Sure cross-country itself is a superb vehicle for cross-training. But you don't need to start edging your ankles in your sleep to attain a level of commitment that could benefit from cross-training aids to your skiing. You don't even need to think in terms of training; think, instead, of cross-conditioning, since it isn't necessary to monitor every physical activity as it might relate to a qualitative training program.

Steve Gaskill, former coach of the U.S. cross-country team, now works with Team Birky, a Minnesota-

based youth and ski development program. His background as an instructor in the sport gives Gaskill a good idea of which activities can aid skiers with varying levels of expertise. Here are some of his suggestions:

Walking with Poles

Sounds simple, but divide the responsibility of movement between arms and legs and you'll prepare your body for the trails with every step. Use poles that roughly reach your sternum, about 65 percent of your total height. The more uphills, the better.

Hiking

Especially on hilly trails, you'll find that as you work your legs, you'll be transferring weight for balance just because of all the uneven footing. Push yourself along with poles, and your stroll will really help your

skating stride and your double-poling. The use of poles in both cross-country skiing and hiking acts as a relief to the legs and back, because

the upper body and arms absorb much of the work.

Distance Running

It may not do much for the arms, but a 10-kilometer run — especially one with hills — will keep your aerobic threshold up and strengthen the legs. Jogs, jaunts, and runs are still great for diagonal striders, whose motion is more linear than skaters'.

Swimming

Here's another chance to increase your cardiovascular base and to work all your muscles without pounding them. The sore-jointed among us love water's forgiving platform. Perfect? Not quite. The problem? "Laterals and abdominals," Gaskill says. "You push through with your lats more in cross-country than you do in swimming.

And even good swimmers need to do something else to work their abdominal muscles."

Roller Skiing vs. In-line Skating

"Top skiers do lots of roller skiing, but very little in-line skating [rollerblading]," says Gaskill. "In-line

wheels go so fast, you really don't develop the musculature that you need for cross-country, which causes more resistance with the snow. Actually, older, cheaper skates will help you more, because they have more slack [resistance]."

Circuit Training

You can go into a health club, toss a few things around, and enhance your body's ability to do most anything. But not every exercise will help every type of athlete. Cross-country skiers are among the lucky ones. Since they use almost every muscle group, they can also derive benefit from more contraptions than most athletes. Anaerobic elements of weight machines can amplify your capacity to perform individual components of the aerobic whole.

Gaskill recalls his days as national team coach, when he would have his charges "do pushes, pulls, dips, frequent light repetitions that added tone instead of bulk to our muscles, not like the guys who work out for show. We would also pull on rubber cords that were similar to ski poles.

"Basically, a cross-country skier's body should encounter moderate, continuous resistance while repeating quick explosive exercises."

Gaskill also recommends a variety of sports from basketball to soccer to gymnastics to racquet sports — "anything that makes you move around and forces you to work your stabilizer and rotator muscles."

Sports requiring detours that are sudden and unplanned — if they don't turn your ankles or pull your muscles — will condition your body for the shifts it will make when it adjusts to changes on the trail.

INJURY PREVENTION

Classic Nordic touring will strain tight hamstrings and quadriceps, especially if recent inactivity has left the muscles like a tangled telephone wire. Daily limbering and pre-trail stretching will help you avert cramps.

The lower back is a common trouble spot for new cross-country skiers, who find themselves hunching forward more than they would like. Sit-ups and back extensions build resistance to wear, if they are done with proper form. Check with your doctor or chiropractor if you plan to ski and either have been inactive or have a history of back pain. There are many ways to do back exercises incorrectly. The best way for you to do them correctly may depend on your health.

Skaters should also try lifting their legs up while lying on their side in order to strengthen the abductor muscles — the gluteus, minimus, and medius — that go to work during the V-1.

GOING FARTHER

So you've decided to turn your strides into a weekend excursion, or perhaps a full week. Maybe you want to bring the family along, see some new ski country, join a club, enter a race — something that gives new expression to your newfound love of cross-country skiing.

A little advance planning will simplify the journey for you and your companions. There are enough options for skiers of all ages and abilities to make a memorable happening out of their time on the snow.

BRINGING THE KIDS

Now that you've learned the joys of cross-country skiing, it's time for your kids to catch the cross-country bug. Given a child's natural enthusiasm for frolicking in the snow, your role as instructor may not be as significant as your role as monitor. You don't need to teach kids to have fun, as long as they're doing it safely.

Fending for Themselves

This may surprise you, but the younger and less experienced the child, the less emphasis should be placed on specified technique. Why? Too complicated. Introductory elements of cross-country skiing should be made as simple as possible, so that children will feel free to make

motion into words. For most children, the first few steps may best be taken without ski poles, which will only encumber them as they try to gain a sense of balance.

Games

The best way to encourage children to practice what is intended as instruction or training is to arrange the activity in the form of a game.

When introducing young children to cross-country skiing, go easy on instruction; they'll teach themselves through trial and error and have more fun in the bargain.

mistakes, experiment, and have fun. Remember, you don't explain to children how to walk; they need to teach themselves through trial and error. Eventually, they gain confidence and can walk across the room, turn around, jump, climb a step, and function on their feet without knowing why. The same idea applies to slightly older children who are learning how to walk on skis. Once the body remembers how to balance itself, the muscles never forget, even if the brain can't quite translate the

Can they walk from one end of the house to the other on skis, for instance?

Once on the snow, children need to gain confidence with the idea of having skis under their feet. On open, flat surfaces, younger children can play games such as follow the leader, although you'll need to make certain the leader isn't much faster than the slowest follower.

Hide and seek is a good game for getting children to feel comfortable walking around bushes and other obstacles, since their friends will

probably be hiding behind them.

By leading children in a game such as Simon says, you can teach them how to transfer their weight from ski to ski. "Simon says stand on the right leg," and so on.

A game of tag will encourage children to move more quickly on skis and will also demystify the act of falling — a given in a game of tag, even without skis. Be prepared to help a fallen child off the ground, but keep in mind that uninstructed children are usually more resourceful than uninstructed adults when it comes to righting themselves. Besides, parental intervention is often the kiss of death to useful instruction, so allow a child to pick

himself up before offering help. In general, monitor closely, but interfere as little as possible, so the child learns to be independent and, ultimately, more confident on skis.

Once children can move around better on skis, games such as soccer, hockey, or dodge ball can teach them how to turn and maintain balance.

All games should be closely supervised, since children often play with abandon once they find that they are having fun. Also remember that children may have boundless enthusiasm, but they don't have the endurance of an adult. Keep an eye out for kids who drag through an activity. If you decide to leave children on their own for a short time,

GEAR TALK

KIDS' CLOTHES

Be sure to dress children as warmly as possible. Toddlers should be clothed in snowsuits until they are able to glide along with purpose. Once they begin to negotiate their own way on skis, start to layer them as you would layer yourself. Be sure to find boots that fit properly, since nothing is more discouraging to an impressionable first-time skier than cold, wet toes. A child's ski package may run between $75 and $100, but there are ways to minimize costs.

Look for hand-me-downs either from a child's older sibling or a friend with a child around the same age. Additionally, some Nordic centers have ski exchanges as an option for parents who would rather not buy new gear once a season for their growing children. Simply turn in whatever your child has outgrown and, for a nominal fee, exchange it for something in a different size. If you make such an exchange, be sure the gear is not too worn for adequate use, and have the child give the new skis, boots, or poles a good test run.

make certain that the leader — the one whose lead the others follow — is responsible enough to watch out for the slower, younger members of the group rather than show off in order to humiliate them.

Rest Periods

It also doesn't hurt to find a way to give children a break once in a while. Give them a piggy-back ride for a few minutes. Put them on a

> 66 The Gods are too airy:
> feathery as the snow
> When its consistency is just the
> imagination's,
> I recognize, but also in an airy,
> gauzy way
> That it will capture me, I will
> never capture it. 99

—Richard Eberhart,
from *Collected Poems*

sled. Give them a chance to rest. Remember, children have far more energy than you do over a short period of time, but they tire more easily.

SLEDS. Infants and small children can fit snugly into sleds that are specially designed for light ski touring. "Pulks" are lightweight fiberglass sleds complete with spray skirts, windshields, and harnesses to keep the children strapped in. They attach firmly to your waist and distribute the pull of the sled in such a way that the children will feel lighter than their actual weight as you are towing them along. Pulks are very specialized equipment and can also be expensive. You may be able to rent one from your local Nordic center, however, for as little as $5 a day, thereby saving both the expense and the inconvenience of buying, storing, and carting your own.

You can also cart an infant along in a backpack carrier, but be sure that you feel stable enough on skis, yourself, before acting as a human pulk. And remember that inactive children need to be closely monitored, since a passive body, particularly a small one, tends to catch cold easily. Make sure that children don't fall asleep while being carried in a backpack.

SENIORS

Senior citizens can not only prolong their lives with a consistent form of physical exercise, they can also derive immense enjoyment from a regular activity that affords them both a cardiovascular workout and a form of social interaction. To this end, cross-country skiing can refresh the heart and soul perfectly.

Craftsbury, Vermont, is one of many towns that run an Elderhostel, a ski program and facility designed exclusively for those in their golden

years. The programs offer discounts on products, courses in physical exercise for seniors, a chance to meet people who are roughly the same age and have similar ability, and, of course, cross-country lessons tailored to meet the needs and expectations of seniors.

"Many seniors see cross-country skiing as a natural extension of walking, but are held back by a fear of falling," says Laurie Gullian, ski author and instructor. "The first thing to learn is to lower your center of gravity or squat and plant a buttock cheek. Don't stick an arm or hand out to break the fall."

How to Start

Gullian points out that some of the games used to familiarize children with the notion of skiing can also work with seniors. A game, for instance, is a good way to encourage older skiers to get used to standing on one leg at a time. For the timid who may be afraid to stand up on skis, she advises starting first on just hands and knees, then sliding one foot forward first in order to feel how the ski will slide along the snow. This is also the preferred method for first-time skiers of any age to right themselves after a fall. It is also possible to remove one ski in order to get up more easily.

Recreational dancers often have an advantage when they ski, because of the coordination, balance, and timing required to maintain step.

Cross-country is a superb winter activity for older citizens, who can either take leisurely strolls on skis or compete, like this septuagenarian.

Some introductory lessons at Elderhostels are, in fact, set to music. So bring a partner, or be prepared to find a new one.

SKI CLUBS AND GUIDES

WHY JOIN A CLUB? Clubs usually allow skiers to find discounts on equipment, events, publications, and

Joining an outing club can be the best way to learn about local backwoods trails while you find companions who ski at your pace.

poorly marked or if you may encounter avalanche zones, guides will tell you how to navigate. For this reason, skiers in the mountainous Rockies are more likely to use a guide than those out for a day-long adventure off the beaten track in the Northeast or Midwest.

other ski-related items. Clubs also serve as a sort of sounding board for ideas about the sport. If you have questions about equipment, facilities, instructors, or out-of-the-way places to ski, you can easily compare notes with other members. You're also bound to find people in the club who ski at your pace, whether you're a beginner or an expert. If you don't have a regular partner who is as fervent about skiing as you are, a ski club is a good place to meet one.

WHY GO WITH A GUIDE? For the inexperienced, the company of a guide takes out the guesswork. Is your journey too difficult? Have you strayed too far? What is the best way to navigate this tricky patch of terrain? Is your form okay? Trained guides are virtually essential if you are planning one of your first trips into the backcountry or have a multi-day excursion ahead. If areas are

CHOOSING A DESTINATION

Regardless of where you go, it is always an advantage to be able to start your day's journey from the comfort of your lodge or inn instead of having to drive to the place from which you take your first strides. When you start from the inn, you can travel lighter and ski in shifts based on your staying power or slight changes in the weather. Perhaps you'd rather ski for an hour here and 45 minutes there. Or maybe you'd like to wait for the snow and heavy winds to die down. There is much less flexibility when you first drive a long distance and then ski away from where you left your car, knowing you still have a long drive back to your lodging at the end of the day.

The Northeast

With terrain featuring rolling hills and wooded trails, the Northeastern states were the region of the initial growth of cross-country skiing in this country. From the hills of southern New England to the challenging mountains of New York State's Adirondacks and New Hampshire's White Mountains, there are beautiful scenic opportunities for the Eastern cross-country skier.

Light outerwear may be an option on some days, but footwear is another matter. Snowshoes are popular in the New England forest and hilly areas more properly suited for hikers than skiers. Because wet snow conditions are common, the use of waxless skis is also more common than in, say, the Rocky Mountains of Colorado, where the air is dry and waxing is an art form. Waxed skis usually perform better than waxless, but only in dry, ideal conditions.

Northeastern cross-country centers are generally accessible from major metropolitan areas. They can be crowded, but are easy to get to for most people, and they are accustomed to catering to beginners. New England inns that maintain their own cross-country trails are a wonderful option for city dwellers looking for a long weekend of skiing along with all the amenities. And for longer yet

GEAR TALK

SKI RACKS

Once you've accounted for every other aspect of your trip, ski transport can be the one overlooked detail that floors you. Shorter skating skis may fit nicely into the back of a station wagon or perhaps you can lay the skis over the seat backs and away from the passengers' heads. But if you have a small car, or simply need the trunk space for other gear, ski racks are a convenient way to carry skis.

Ski racks, available for virtually every model car, have been the preferred choice over the past 10 to 15 years. You could instead purchase a cargo carrier, which allows you to transport additional gear. On a rack, skis will be exposed to the elements at highway speeds, but that isn't likely to harm them any more than using them on the snow. Still, if you want to protect skis and poles, molded plastic containers are available that mount on top of the ski rack. A "space case" is a cargo carrier that mounts on top and splits in half the way a suitcase would. The case has a shell covering for skis and poles to keep them protected from weather and covered for security reasons.

Ski touring below Fairy Castle Ridge, Bryce Canyon National Park, southwestern Utah. As national parks become overrun with people, exploring them in winter is an appealing option.

similarly comfortable outings, there are also packaged inn-to-inn tours.

The Upper Midwest

Weather you travel to cities or take in a trail on one of the region's vast public lands, you're likely to find a park, a trail, a meadow, a golf course or some bustling or quiet cross-country ski spot with your name on

SKI FEST

Each year, cross-country ski areas, retailers, suppliers, and ski publications unite to present "Ski Fest — a celebration of cross-country skiing." The annual event, tailored to the needs of the beginning skier, incorporates more than 200 ski areas and 500 specialty retail stores and enables more than 40,000 skiers to receive free ski lessons, complimentary access to Nordic centers, discounted trail passes for return visits, and considerable discounts on equipment. Ski Fest activities include ski games for children, equipment demonstrations, trailside snacks, prize drawings, and even golf on skis. Check with Ski Industries America, 703-556-9020, for a list of participating ski areas.

it. First-time skiers will appreciate the long, flat terrain — as opposed to the mountainous Rockies or the undulating New England terrain — often with no more than 4 or 5 inches of snow on level ground. It is terrain well suited for those who just want to take off and hit their stride. If you venture into what forested wilderness exists, be sure that you or a companion can properly orient your group.

Attire can often be on the light side, but beware the changeability of temperature and have enough flexibility in your layering scheme to adjust accordingly. Remember, open, level fields do not have trees around to break the wind, which can be strong in the Upper Midwest.

The Rockies

The state of Colorado boasts the longest ski season of any U.S. state except Alaska. During spring and autumn months, you are still likely to

---

BILL KOCH YOUTH SKI LEAGUE

Better known simply as the Bill Koch League, this is cross-country skiing's largest official membership group in the United States (3,000+ skiers in 100+ clubs). It offers cross-country and ski-jumping programs to youngsters age 13 and younger.

The League consists of local clubs sponsored by schools, touring centers, and larger ski clubs. The clubs generally meet several times a week to hold clinics, meetings, or special events. Once or twice each season, at least one club within a given geographical region will hold a mini-festival, involving up to 500 skiers.

The Bill Koch League was founded, in the words of its mission statement, "to introduce young people to the lifelong sport of skiing with its recreational, social, fitness and competitive opportunities."

For the annual membership fee of $15, participants receive a membership card, stickers, patches, and a subscription to the club's national newsletter, as well as many discounts on books, videotapes, and other items.

Through the club's "K for Kochers" awards program, skiers receive patches based upon their age and hours spent on skis.

Those wishing more information may write to:
USA/BKYSL
P.O. Box 100
Park City, UT 84060
or call 801-649-9090.

find breathtaking views of mountain-tops with snow underfoot. For those who like to use wax, the conditions are often easier to read in the Rockies than in the Northeast, where snow conditions are at the mercy of the region's notoriously unpredictable weather.

The number of touring centers in the region has increased rapidly over the last decade, but not quite fast enough to meet the demand. Novice skiers often must make a long drive to find an uncluttered spot that suits them. Many places near the larger resorts have less-than-ideal condi-tions: chippy ice, terrain that is both steep and wavy, and masses of people with the same idea as yours.

The vast backcountry makes Colorado a great spot for the experi-enced skier, and it takes numerous visits to appreciate the varied land-scape fully. But veterans and neo-phytes alike need to be aware of avalanche hazards associated with the high mountains. Dress warmly enough to withstand the cold, dry air, and always listen to weather fore-casts. Travel in a group whenever possible.

The Pacific Northwest

The Seattle/Vancouver area is famous for its rain. The wet, heavy snowpack makes waxing tricky. The footing is often discouraging to young skiers during most of the year, and the optimal seasons are short on both sides of the Cascades, which, in

effect, serve as the demarcation line for snow conditions. On the east side, the dry snow is best navigated between mid-December and early March. The west side, where freezing rain literally puts a damper on the winter season, is the place to go during the succeeding spring and early summer months, when the slush adopts a corn consistency favored by many experienced skiers.

There are plenty of touring cen-ters in the region, so you should be able to find what you like within a comfortable drive.

Northern California & The Sierras

The snowfalls are significant, but the season is brief, because the weather does not stay cold for very long. There are enough good forest areas during the ski season, but open, flatter terrain for youngsters and seniors is less plentiful. Beware of the masses of snow that form soggy blotches during the warmer late winter months.

If you like corn-snow skiing, the east side of the Sierras is excellent, with a spring ski season that allows you to tour at high elevations before breathtaking views while you wear only light clothing. Expect to see some people skiing in shorts.

Enjoy the warm weather, but bring sunglasses and a strong sun-screen! Remember, as you gain ele-vation, the ultraviolet rays become stronger.

RESORTS

Whereas the destination traveler drives the alpine ski industry, cross-country skiers are less likely to plan a ski holiday with all the trimmings. But there are cross-country-oriented ski resorts available, with amenities from modest to lavish.

Resorts not only provide lodging, equipment, advice, maps, lessons, and the use of groomed trails for a flat price, but they also have a variety of restaurants, tours, and entertainment. Nordic skiers may see this option as part of the alpine mentality they would like to avoid, but it certainly exists.

Places to Go

Royal Gorge, California, hosts the world's largest cross-country ski resort, with 9,000 acres of skiing terrain and over 300 kilometers of groomed track overlooking the breathtaking Sierra Nevada mountains.

In Waterville Valley, New Hampshire, skiers can test their skills on 105 kilometers of trails that cut through forest, fields, and streams and eventually lead into the White Mountain National Forest. You can utilize the ski instructors or try your hand at the racing loops, which cover 5 kilometers.

The Home Ranch, a dude ranch in northern Colorado, conducts a ski tour complete with lessons, entertainment, and amenities. C Lazy U Ranch in Granby, Colorado, is another such resort.

Even traditional alpine resorts such as California's Diamond Peak, Kirkwood, and Northstar have expanded to include cross-country programs. *Cross-Country Skier* magazine offers an annual "Travelers' Guide" to the best resorts and touring centers around the country.

CITIZEN RACES

There is no better way for a cross-country skier to test the stamina of mind and body than to enter a marathon citizen race. If you have ever run or biked a marathon, you know how strong the simultaneous feelings of invigorating achievement and debilitating fatigue are. Still, you should always be physically trained for a race of any distance and should always ski within your limits.

Citizen races need not be marathons. Although the larger, more popular races generally cover marathon (50-kilometer) distances and beyond, most races run between 5 and 15 kilometers and serve as social carnivals for the towns in which they are held. The emphasis is on winning for only a select few. For most, the goal is simply to finish, perhaps to ski slightly faster than in the last race. The atmosphere is one of encouragement and cooperation. Spectators line the race route to cheer, while volunteers offer refreshments, quick medical attention, minor gear repair, and other assistance. On days when you couldn't

Citizen races of between 5 and 15 kilometers are a great way to test your stamina. The atmosphere at such events is encouraging and friendly.

Be sure to wax properly. This is a standard pre-race parking-lot ritual. Give your skis a good test run, checking uphills for grip. Stash spare wax in a fanny pack in case snow conditions change.

possibly cover the given distance of a citizen race by yourself, the assembled supporters can will you across the finish line. Most people who ski the races just for fun have a blast no matter what their finishing time.

Race Day Logistics

Make sure you arrive early to give yourself time to stretch (see "Loosening Up to Ski," page 59). The longer the race and the colder the temperature, the more time you need to spend stretching your muscles. If you've picked up your race bib ahead of time, make sure you don't forget to bring it. If you need to pay the fee on race day, make sure you bring enough money with you to cover it. You may also want to stash some spare change in a pocket so you can phone somebody if you happen to drop out near a place that has a phone.

Be sure to use the bathroom as close to race time as possible. You will, no doubt, want to make sure you are well hydrated before the race, and should probably increase your fluid intake a day before the race even if you don't feel thirsty. But until you start moving, be aware of the nearest pit stop.

WARM-UP. Stretch as you would for a long day's ski tour. Then stop, take a deep breath, and stretch some more. The euphoria of a race will likely carry you through rough patches that might have caused you to stop during a normal tour. That may be fine for your oxygen tank, but bad for your hamstrings. Even if you feel limber, be sure to stay loose.

Match Your Pace

Large race fields should have pace times lining the start area. Finding one that is equal to your anticipated

finish time will make the crowded first kilometer a lot smoother. If skiers of similar ability ski in the same area, the faster skiers don't end up pushing to the front in order to pass the slower skiers. In smaller races that don't have pace times listed, ask a few competitors what time they expect to finish. Try to find a few skiers with times similar to yours, and start near them. There is nothing more encumbering in a group race than a slowpoke who clogs the front or a speed demon who charges from the back. Be aware that mass starts can be tricky. Search for a spot near your given pace with a little bit of elbow room, and shake yourself around to avoid muscle tightness as you wait for the signal to ski. Be prepared to jockey for position once the race starts.

MID-RACE FUEL. Just because you're racing doesn't mean you shouldn't fill your fuel tank, even if you have to stop and watch people pass while you do it. In the long run, that sip of sports drink or bite of candy bar will

SKIING FOR THE DISABLED

There is no need to associate physical handicaps with physical inactivity, even for those who wish to ski. Disabled skiers are hitting the trails in increasing numbers, and those classified as "amputee" and "sight-impaired" have their own national teams. There is even a third class of disabled skiers — paraplegics — who have the benefit of new, albeit expensive, equipment that can allow them to ski. "Virtually anybody who wants to ski can do it," says Kendall Butz, coach of the U.S. Disabled Nordic Team. "You need to have patience, realistic expectations, and the willingness to work at it. That's true for skiers with and without disabilities."

AMPUTEES. Skiers who use leg prosthetics that don't go as high as the knee can often get by very nicely by using the same techniques that an able-bodied skier uses. Those with prosthetics that begin above the knee will probably have to rely on the kick double-pole. Butz points out that amputees often need to exaggerate their weight shift in order to get the necessary kick from their amputee side. "Skiing is skiing," Butz says. "You may not get as strong a kick. It is harder to push off with three limbs than four, but it's no less rewarding."

Arm amputees will either use one pole or no poles. Even those athletes with one arm sometimes elect to forgo the use of a single

continued on next page

pole, because some find that it throws off their balance.

THE SIGHT-IMPAIRED. Butz says that Rule 1 for the sight-impaired is to find a club or ski area that will help locate a good qualified guide. The guide will assist the sight-impaired skier either by leading or following him around the trail. It is very important for the blind skier to develop a good relationship with the guide.

"For blind skiers, the most common obstacles are balance and trust. It's a different type of movement, and once skiers feel themselves sliding instead of shuffling, they've already begun to trust their guides, their skis, and themselves."

PARAPLEGICS. For those who have lost all use of their legs but can still use their arms, there are new adjustable skis made to compensate for their disability. The skis are mounted either on bolts or on a binding system located roughly 8 inches off the snow, and skiers move the apparatus by double-poling. For negotiating turns, the skis are equipped with an adjustable articulator that adapts the skis to the curves in the grooves of the tracks and moves the skier around accordingly. Essentially, the articulator controls the tension needed to turn the skis. Paraplegic skiers need to have very strong arms in order to climb anything more than slight uphills. They can use a pole drag to help control speed on the downhills.

do more good than harm to both you and your finish time.

Finish Plans

Regardless of race length, it's always good to have someone meet you at the finish area. First of all, your achievement will be more meaningful if you can share it with a friend or relative. Second, your party can always carry additional food, clothing changes and Ben-Gay. Even if you have your own car handy near the

finish area, you probably won't feel like driving after a taxing race.

Remember, you will need to have two plans: one in case you finish, and the other in case you drop out mid-race. Be sure to establish the specific spot where you plan to meet someone, especially in a crowded race. Find out from race organizers which entrances and exits will be accessible to entrants and spectators.

If you need to drop out several miles from the finish, make sure you

have a way to get back to your destination or a way to contact somebody who can pick you up. Many ski marathons run through main streets of towns, where telephones are but a few strides away. But to be safe, you should operate under the assumption that you may need to stop where phone booths are infrequent and your mobility is limited because of fatigue, blisters, or equipment malfunction. Remember, if slowing down will help you finish, don't let your pride get the better of you. Slow down or stop.

After the Race

Once you've crossed the finish line, be sure to get inside, change out of

JUHA MIETO

Though few people remember his name, Juha Mieto's imposing, robust image made him the Herculean poster man for cross-country skiing in the 1970s. Listed modestly at 6 feet 7 inches and 240 pounds, Mieto was a gracious, gentle Finnish giant who somehow acquired an extra helping of shoulders at birth. He began shaving at age 12, and at 17 sported a full beard no one ever told him to cut.

In competition, passing flakes took such a liking to his facial hair that by mid-race, beard and bib would be one inseparable frosty garb.

Mieto was the quintessential Nordic skier, and a French journalist once remarked that he could make the weather change when he entered a room. "Instead of muscles," the scribe penned, "he has profound ridges you can climb."

In his first Winter Games at Sapporo in 1972, Mieto missed a bronze medal in the 15-kilometer race by 6/100 second. Four years later in Innsbruck, he took fourth once more — by 11 seconds — in the 30-kilometer.

In 1980, vowing never to be fourth again, Mieto won his first two individual medals, both silvers, at the Lake Placid Olympic Games. This time, in the 15-kilometer he collapsed across the finish line in a valiant bid for the gold, and because of the race's staggered start, had to wait for his foes' results while mending in a medical tent. Mieto's time (47 minutes, 57.64 seconds) held up until Sweden's Thomas Wassberg overtook it by 1/100 second. The margin of victory, about the length of a snowflake, was so infinitesimal that ski officials decided thereafter to time races in tenths of a second at major international events.

In citizen races, try to find a few skiers with times similar to yours and start near them. Be prepared to jockey for position once the race begins.

your wet clothes, and warm up. It's a good idea to have a cup of hot chocolate on hand when you plop into the tub. You've earned it. Be sure to maintain your fluid intake, and remember that stretching after a race can be as important as stretching beforehand. It's a good way to soothe the lactic acid out of your legs. Name-brand sport creams are fine, but should not be considered a substitute for stretching and massaging tired muscles.

SOURCES & RESOURCES

No book can meet the needs of every reader. However, in an attempt to further assist you in your quest for a memorable cross-country ski experience, we have compiled a lengthy list of names and addresses for organizations, guides, and ski centers, as well as suggestions for reading, viewing, and purchasing. Read on.

ON-LINE SERVICES (The Internet)

The Internet is a powerful place to get started. There is an enormous amount of information available, but it can mean spending hours sifting through dozens of Web sites. For specific information, however, it can't be beat. Web addresses listed for associations, guides, ski centers, schools, and commercial sites also have useful links. Services and information available

through the Internet change rapidly, but these are additional sites we can recommend at the time of publication.

www.gorp.com—Web links, destinations, ski events, trips, tours, gear, apparel, clubs.

www.goski.com—links to Nordic/cross-country skiing resources on the Internet.

www.madnorski.org—Nordic skiing links on every subject imaginable.

www.skicentral.com—a clearinghouse for thousands of ski sites.

www.skiingadventures.com—a Gordon's Guide comprehensive directory of cross-country ski lodges in the U.S. and Canada.

www.ski-injury.com—information on the incidence, causes, and prevention of Nordic and Telemark ski injuries.

www.skitele.com—for the Telemark skiing community.

www.snowreport.com—features a quick snow search.

www.telemarktips.com—Telemark and backcountry skiing Webzine.

www.trailsource.com—on-line guide to cross-country trails worldwide with great links.

www.xcountryski-vermont .com—an authoritative cross-country ski report for Vermont with lots of useful links.

www.xcski.org—site of the Cross Country Ski Areas Association, with lots of directories and information about events and services.

www.zocho.com—on-line sports directory with lots of Nordic sites.

ASSOCIATIONS

Associations are eager to promote their sport and can often provide lists of local groups or individuals that you may contact.

AMERICAN BLIND SKIING FOUNDATION

163 Walnut Street
Elmhurst, IL 60126
www.absf.org
E-mail: absf@bigfoot.com
Organizes downhill and cross-country ski lessons and competitions for the blind and visually handicapped.

AMERICAN CROSS COUNTRY SKIERS

P.O. Box 604
Bend, OR 97709
888-543-7223
www.xcskiworld.com
Dedicated to tack skiing, light touring, and racing; Web site features advice, events, information on equipment and training, and destinations.

BILL KOCH YOUTH SKI LEAGUE

Over 100 local clubs which promote cross-country skiing events and instruction. Find out more through your local ski area, or contact NENSA (see below) for clubs in New England.

CROSS COUNTRY SKI AREAS ASSOCIATION

259 Bolton Road
Winchester, NH 03470
603-239-4341
www.xcski.org
E-mail: ccsaa@xcski.org
Lists hundreds of U.S. and Canadian cross-country ski areas and trails. Web site features snow reports and information on events, equipment, and destinations.

NEW ENGLAND NORDIC SKI ASSOCIATION (NENSA)

P.O. Box 176
Fairfax, VT 05454
802-849-2270
www.nensa.net
Sanctioning body for most New England Nordic skiing events, hosting competitive, educational, participation-based activities across the Northeast.

NORTH AMERICAN TELEMARK ORGANIZATION

P.O. Box 44
Waitsfield, VT 05673
800-835-3404
www.telemarknato.com
E-mail: info@telemarknato.com
Offers Telemark instructional clinics, workshops, camps, and adventure tours.

PACIFIC NORTHWEST SKI ASSOCIATION (PNSA)

3414 228th St. SE
Bothell, WA 98021
425-483-8666
www.pnsa.org
E-mail: pnsa@pnsa.org
Promotes all types of skiing and ski competitions for individuals in northern Idaho, Oregon, and Washington state. Web site lists regional calendar of events and Nordic ski clubs.

PROFESSIONAL SKI INSTRUCTORS OF AMERICA

133 South Van Gordon Street, Suite 101
Lakewood, CO 80228
303-987-9390
www.psia.org
Organization for ski instructors providing training and certification through regional divisions. Answers questions about ski areas, ski schools, and ski equipment.

SKI FOR LIGHT

1455 West Lake Street
Minneapolis, MN 55408
612-827-3232
www.sfl.org
E-mail: info@sfl.org
Helps organize cross-country skiing programs for visually impaired and other physically disabled people.

SNOWSPORTS INDUSTRIES AMERICA

8377-B Greensboro Drive
McLean, VA 22102
703-556-9020
www.snowsports.org
E-mail: siamail@snowsports.org
National, nonprofit trade association representing more than 800 on-snow product manufacturers, distributors, and suppliers.

U.S. BIATHLON ASSOCIATION

29 Ethan Allen Avenue
Colchester, VT 05446
800-242-8456 or 802-654-7833
www.usbiathlon.org
E-mail: usbiathlon@aol.com
The national governing body for biathlon in the U.S.

U.S. DEAF SKI AND SNOWBOARD ASSOCIATION

0400 SW Palatine Hill Road
Portland, OR 97219-6551
www.usdssa.org
Promotes recreational and competitive skiing and snowboarding for the deaf and hearing impaired in the U.S.

U.S. SKI AND SNOWBOARD ASSOCIATION (USSA)

P.O. Box 100
1500 Kearns Blvd.
Park City, UT 84060
435-649-9090
www.ussa.org
E-mail: special2@ussa.org
The governing body for Olympic Nordic and alpine skiing and snowboarding in the U.S., fielding and maintaining teams of world-class ski athletes.

WORLD MASTERS CROSS-COUNTRY SKI ASSOCIATION

USA Headquarters
P.O. Box 5
Bend, OR 97709
541-382-3503
www.world-masters-xc-skiing.ch
E-mail: dhuntwm@coinet.com
Promotes masters cross-country skiing worldwide.

WORLD LOPPET/AMERICAN BIRKEBEINER

P.O. Box 911
Hayward, WI 54843
800-872-2753 or 715-634-5025
www.worldloppet.com
E-mail: birkie@birkie.com
International sports federation of cross-country skiing marathons around the world, recently united 14 races from Europe, America, Asia, and Australia. American Birkebeiner is North America's largest cross-country ski marathon.

GUIDES (Including Hut-to-Hut opportunities)

The organizations and guides below offer a variety of trips at all levels. For more listings, check out the back pages of Nordic skiing magazines or look on the Web.

ADIRONDACK MOUNTAIN SCHOOL

P.O. Box 248
Keene, NY 12942
518-576-2242
www.adkmtschool.com
E-mail: jesse@adkmtschool.com
Backcountry ski expeditions, introductory backcountry tours, summit ski tours, classic trails and multi-day mountaineering adventures in the High Peaks region.

ALPINE SKILLS INTERNATIONAL

P.O. Box 8
Norden, CA 95724
530-426-9108
www.alpineskills.com
E-mail: info@alpineskills.com
Backcountry tours that range from mild to wild, with self-guided Nordic trips and custom trips individually arranged.

ASPEN ALPINE GUIDES, INC.

P.O. Box 659
Aspen, CO 81612
800-643-8621 or 970-925-6618
www.aspenalpine.com
E-mail: skiguides@attbi.com
Year-round guide service in the Aspen area offering backcountry hut trips and ski mountaineering for all ability levels.

CAMPALASKA TOURS

P.O. Box 872247
Wasilla, AK 99687
800-376-9438 or 907-376-9438
www.campalaska.com
E-mail: info@campalaska.com
Cross-country skiing and dogsledding in Alaska.

METHOW VALLEY BACKCOUNTRY

Rendezvous Huts Inc.
P.O. Box 728
Winthrop, WA 98862
509-996-8100
www.methow.com/huts/info.html
E-mail: heitman@methow.com
Self-guided hut-to-hut tours available, or Rendezvous Huts will organize a 2 to 5 day back-country trip.

MOUNTAIN MADNESS

4218 South West Alaska,
Suite 206
Seattle, WA 98116
206-937-8389
www.mountainmadness.com
E-mail:
info@mountainmadness.com
Organizes 6-day Crater Lake ski tours for novices as well as advanced skiers.

SIERRA WILDERNESS SEMINARS, INC.

11080 SW Allen Blvd.,
Suite 500-D
Beaverton, OR 97005
888-797-6867 or 503-626-3006
www.swsmtns.com
E-mail: mail@swsmtns.com
REI's northern California wilderness school offering back-country skiing in exotic places, including California!

TENTH MOUNTAIN DIVISION HUT ASSOCIATION

1280 Ute Avenue, Suite 21
Aspen, CO 81611
970-925-5775
www.huts.org
E-mail: huts@huts.org
Maintains 29 well-equipped huts along a 350-mile network of ski routes atop the Rocky Mountains. Reserve a hut and ski on your own, or contact the Tenth Mountain Division Hut Association about a guided tour.

YOSEMITE CROSS COUNTRY SKI SCHOOL

Yosemite Park and Curry Company
Yosemite National Park, CA 95389
209-372-8444
www.yosemiteparktours.com
Offers a 6-day trans-Sierra crossing, across the Tioga Pass and down to Yosemite Valley. Skiers will snow camp or stay in alpine huts.

NORDIC SKI CENTERS

These are some recommendations for resorts that can give you a complete package. The number of Nordic ski centers is rapidly increasing and you will find advertisements in the back of magazines or by searching the Internet.

IN THE EASTERN UNITED STATES

BEARSKIN LODGE
124 East Bearskin Road
Grand Marais, MN 55604
800-338-4170 or 218-388-2292
www.bearskin.com
E-mail: stay@bearskin.com
Relatively flat terrain and numerous frozen waterways allow you to ski on or off 30 miles of groomed trails in a true wilderness area.

BLUEBERRY HILL INN
Goshen, VT 05733
802-247-6735
www.blueberryhillinn.com
E-mail:
info@blueberryhillinn.com
75 kilometers of groomed and wilderness trails, including the highest maintained ski trail in Vermont and other routes for self-reliant backcountry skiers.

BOLTON VALLEY RESORT
4302 Bolton Access Road
Bolton, VT 05477
877-926-5866 or 802-434-3444
www.boltonvalley.com
E-mail: info@boltonvalley.com
65 miles of trails running through pristine, wooded terrain, with trailside condos and a lodge for accommodation.

GARLAND RESORT
4700 North Red Oak
Lewiston, MI 49756
877-442-7526 or 989-786-2211
www.garlandusa.com
40 miles of groomed cross-country ski trails with resort accommodations.

GUNFLINT TRAIL ASSOCIATION
P.O. Box 205
Grand Marais, MN 55604
800-338-6932
www.gunflint-trail.com
E-mail: gta@gunflint-trail.com
A network of lodges offering four separate cross-country trail systems that extend into the Boundary Waters Canoe Area.

JACKSON SKI TOURING FOUNDATION
P.O. Box 216
Jackson, NH 03846
603-383-9355
www.jacksonxc.org
E-mail: info@jacksonxc.org
A community-based organization maintaining 154 kilometers of groomed cross-country ski trails in and around the village of Jackson, NH, and branching off into the nearby White Mountain National Forest.

MOUNT VAN HOEVENBERG CROSS-COUNTRY CENTER
Verizon Sports Complex
Route 73 at Mt. Van
Hoevenberg
Lake Placid, NY 12946
800-462-6236 or 518-523-2811
www.orda.org
E-mail: vanhoxc@capital.net
35 miles of Olympic-quality trails groomed for both classical and skating techniques with terrain for both novice and expert skiers and 13 racing loops for all levels.

MOUNTAIN TOP INN & RESORT
195 Mountain Top Road
Chittenden, VT 05737
800-445-2100 or 802-483-2311
www.mountaintopinn.com
E-mail:
info@mountaintopinn.com
Offers training seminars and 110 miles of trails, and many other recreational options.

TRAVERSE CITY
Grand Traverse Convention and Visitors Bureau
101 West Grandview Parkway
Traverse City, MI 49684
800-872-8377 or 231-947-1120
www.mytraversecity.com
E-mail: fdbk@traverse.com
A Nordic area with hundreds of miles of groomed public and private trails with nine nearby Nordic resorts.

VERMONT SKI AREAS ASSOCIATION
26 State Street
P.O. Box 368
Montpelier, VT 05601
802-233-2439
www.skivermont.com
E-mail: info@skivermont.com
Comprehensive list of 25 nordic ski areas throughout Vermont.

WATERVILLE VALLEY CROSS COUNTRY
1 Ski Area Road
P.O. Box 540
Waterville Valley, NH 03215
800-468-2553 or 603-236-4666
www.waterville.com
E-mail:
mseeger.wv@boothcreek.com
105km of trails, Telemark and backcountry. Accommodations and numerous recreational activities.

IN THE WESTERN UNITED STATES

ASPEN LODGE
6120 Highway 7
Longs Peak Route
Estes Park, CO 80517
800-332-6867 or 970-586-8133
www.ranchweb.com/aspenlodge
A resort which offers both groomed private trails and truly wild backcountry skiing in the heart of Rocky Mountain National Park.

BUSTERBACK RANCH
Star Route
Ketchum, ID 83340
208-774-2217
30 miles of flat and hilly trails and old-fashioned hospitality.

C LAZY U RANCH
P.O. Box 379
Granby, CO 80446
970-887-3344
www.clazyu.com
E-mail: ranch@clazyu.com
Backcountry and Telemarking trails for guests, with equipment rentals, lessons, guides, and an excellent children's program.

DEVIL'S THUMB RANCH RESORT

P.O. Box 750
Tabermash, CO 80478
800-933-4339 or 970-726-8231
www.rkymtnhi.com/devthumb
E-mail:
devthumb@rkymtnhi.com
40 kilometers of trails at an elevation of over 8,500 feet with deep powder and sunny skies.

DIAMOND PEAK CROSS-COUNTRY

1210 Ski Way
Incline Village, NV 89451
800-468-2463 or 775-832-1177
www.diamondpeak.com
E-mail: info@diamondpeak.com
High above Lake Tahoe, offers equipment rentals and lessons.

HOME RANCH

P.O. Box 822
54880 RCR 129
Clark, CO 80428
970-879-1780
www.homeranch.com
E-mail: info@homeranch.com
Intermediate, hilly terrain as well as meadows for beginners, with accommodations and activities for families.

KIRKWOOD CROSS-COUNTRY SKI AREA

P.O. Box 1
Kirkwood, CA 95646
209-258-6000
www.skikirkwood.com
E-mail: info@kirkwood.com
80km of cross-country trails, including skating lanes, with lodging and family activities available.

LAKEVIEW SKI RANCH

Monida Star Route
Lima, MT 59739
406-276-3278
Various ski touring adventures, including hut-to-hut and Telemarking in remote bowls, accessed by helicopter. Downhill skiing also available.

METHOW VALLEY SPORTS TRAILS ASSOCIATION

MVSTA
P.O. Box 147
Winthrop, WA 98862
509-996-3860
www.mvsta.com
E-mail: info@mvsta.com
Maintains a trail system nearly 200 kilometers in size that spans three distinct cross-country ski areas in the Methow Valley.

MONTECITO-SEQUOIA CROSS-COUNTRY SKI CENTER

1485 Redwood Drive
Los Altos, CA 94024
800-227-9900
www.montecitosequoia.com
E-mail: info@mslodge.com
With 50 miles of trails running between Sequoia and Kings Canyon National Parks, this is a good choice for a strong backcountry skier or a beginner.

MOUNT BACHELOR NORDIC CENTER

P.O. Box 1031
Bend, OR 97709
800-829-2442 or 541-382-1709
www.mtbachelor.com
E-mail: info@mtbachelor.com
This is the spring training center for the U.S. Nordic Ski Team. With 56 miles of ideal racer-in-training tracks and loops, they also offer backcountry skiing in the Cascades.

NORTHSTAR CROSS-COUNTRY AND TELEMARK

P.O. Box 129
Truckee, CA 96160
800-466-6784 or 530-562-1010
www.skinorthstar.com
E-mail:
northstar@boothcreek.com
65km of groomed trails, with equipment rentals, lessons, lodging, and many family activities.

ROYAL GORGE NORDIC SKI RESORT

P.O. Box 1100
9411 Hilside Drive
Soda Springs, CA 95728
800-500-3871 or
800-666-3871 in N. CA
www.royalgorge.com
E-mail: info@royalgorge.com
317km of groomed tracks in the Sierra Nevada, this is the biggest cross-country resort in the U.S. Excellent facilities and ski school.

AND IN CANADA

MONT-SAINTE-ANNE, QUEBEC

2000, Boulevard Beau Pre,
C.P. 400
Beaupre, Quebec,
Canada G0A 1E0
800-463-1568 or 418-827-4561
www.mont-sainte-anne.com
E-mail:
info@mont-sainte-anne.com
223 kilometers of classic skiing trails, 125 kilometers of skating trails along with seven warming huts just a few miles from Old World Quebec City.

WELLS GRAY PROVINCIAL PARK

Wells Gray Chalets &
Wilderness Adventures
P.O. Box 188
Clearwater, British Columbia
Canada V0E 1N0
888-754-8735 or 250-587-6444
www.skihike.com
E-mail: info@skihike.com
Offers both groomed trails and backcountry routes and either guided or unguided tours. Snowcats and helicopters can also drop you off for a real backcountry adventure.

SCHOOLS

Following are just a few places that teach the skills described in this book. For more ideas, contact any of the guides and outfitters listed above.

ELDERHOSTEL
11 Avenue de Lafayette
Boston, MA 02111
877-426-8056 or 978-323-4141
www.elderhostel.org
E-mail:
registration@elderhostel.org
*Programs for older people which
often have an outdoor sports
component, including cross-
country skiing.*

**HURRICANE ISLAND
OUTWARD BOUND**
75 Mechanic Street
Rockland, ME 04841
866-746-9771 or 207-594-5548
www.hurricaneisland.com
E-mail:
info@hurricaneisland.org
*Their winter program includes
all aspects of winter travel.*

**NATIONAL OUTDOOR
LEADERSHIP SCHOOL (NOLS)**
284 Lincoln Street
Lander, WY 82520
800-710-6657 or 307-332-5300
www.nols.edu
E-mail: admissions@nols.edu
*NOLS trains future guides, year-
round, even for college credit, all
over the world.*

FIRST AID TRAINING

**AMERICAN AVALANCHE
INSTITUTE**
P.O. Box 308
Wilson, WY 83014
307-733-3315
www.avalanchecourse.com
E-mail: aai@wyoming.com
Avalanche safety.

**AMERICAN RED CROSS
NATIONAL HEADQUARTERS**
431 18th Street N.W.
Washington, D.C. 20006
800-797-8022 or 202-737-8300
www.redcross.org
E-mail: info@usa.redcross.org
*For first aid and CPR classes
call the American Red Cross and
ask for local chapter information.*

**STONEHEARTH OPEN
LEARNING OPPORTUNITIES,
INC. (SOLO)**
P.O. Box 3150
Conway, NH 03818
603-447-6711
www.soloschools.com
E-mail: info@soloschools.com
*Wilderness and emergency medi-
cine courses.*

**WILDERNESS MEDICAL
ASSOCIATES**
189 Dudley Road
Bryant Pond, ME 04219
888-945-3633 or 207-665-2707
www.wildmed.com
E-mail: office@wildmed.com
*Training specialists in emergency
medicine and wilderness rescue.*

BOOKS
Ah, the perfect accompaniment
for a quiet après-ski evening.
Good books are food for your
spirit.

GEARING UP AND WAXING
*The Complete Guide to Cross-
Country Ski Preparation*, Nat
Brown and Natalie Brown-
Gutnik. 1999. $18.95. Moun-
taineers Books. A complete,
hands-on guide to the tools and
techniques for preparing skis for
optimal performance.

*Waxing and Care of Cross-
Country Skis*, 2nd ed., Michael
Brady and Leif Torgersen. 2001.
$11.95. Wilderness Press. A
guide full of clear photographs
and drawings, with new ways to
make ski care faster and easier.

DOWNHILLS AND TURNS
*Free-Heel Skiing: Telemark and
Parallel Techniques for All Conditions*, Paul Parker. 2001, 3rd
ed. $19.95. Mountaineers
Books. Downhill techniques for
the Nordic skier and information on the latest equipment.

*Allen and Mike's Really Cool
Telemark Tips*, Allen O'Bannon.
1998. $12.95. Falcon Pub-
lishing. Over 100 clear, concise
Telemark tips are comple-
mented by hilarious and helpful
illustrations written for beginners and experts alike.

WORLD OF SKATING
*Ski Skating with Champions:
How to Ski with Least Energy*,
Einar Svensson. 1995. $39.95.
A comprehensive how-to text on
the technique of ski skating.

BACKCOUNTRY SKIING
AMC Guide to Winter Camping,
Stephen Gorman. 1991. Out of
print, but used copies are available for this classic. Appalachian
Mountain Club Books. In addition to treating gear and technique, this guide includes sections on topics such as group
dynamics and leadership, and
camping with children.

Backcountry Skier, Jean Vives.
1998. $18.95. Human Kinetics
publishers.

*Backcountry Skiing Adventures:
Classic Ski and Snowboard
Tours in Vermont and New York*,
David Goodman. 2001. $14.95.
Appalachian Mountain Club
Books.

*Staying Alive in Avalanche
Terrain*, Bruce Tremper. 2001.
$17.95. Mountaineers Books.
Knowledge shared from a professional with 25 years of
avalanche experience.

*Wilderness Skiing and Winter
Camping*, Chris Townsend.
1996. $17.95. Ragged Mountain
Press. A comprehensive guide
covering equipment and
clothing, staying warm, reading
the snow, navigating in bliz-
zards, and more.

WINTER SAFETY

ABC of Avalanche Safety, Edward R. LaChapelle. 2nd ed. 1985. $6.95. Mountaineers Books. A concise, pocket-sized guide to introduce the backcountry user to the basics of avalanche safety.

Avalanche Handbook, David McClung and Peter Schaerer. 2nd ed. 1993. $19.95. Mountaineers Books.

Hypothermia, Frostbite and Other Cold Injuries: Prevention, Recognition and Prehospital Treatment, James A. Wilkerson, C. C. Bangs, and J. S. Hayward. 1986. $12.95. Mountaineers Books.

Medicine for Mountaineering and Other Wilderness Activities, James A. Wilkerson, ed. 5th ed. 2001. $19.95. Mountaineers Books.

Medicine for the Backcountry, Buck Tilton and Frank Hubbell. 3rd ed. 1999. $14.95. Globe Pequot Press.

FITNESS FACTOR

Fitness Cross-Country Skiing, Steven E. Gaskill. 1998. $15.95. Human Kinetics Publishers. Includes 58 color-coded workouts and three sample training programs to challenge skiers according to their fitness and skiing abilities.

Long Distance: Testing the Limits of Body and Spirit in a Year of Living Strenuously, Bill McKibben. 2001. $14.00. Plume Books. Essayist, journalist, and author McKibben decides in his late thirties to test his body through training for competitive cross-country skiing.

Stretching, Bob Anderson. 2nd ed. 2000. $15.95. Shelter Publications, Inc.

GOING FARTHER

Cross Country Northeast: A Guide to the Best Cross-country Skiing Area and Inns of New England and New York, John R. Fitzgerald. 1994. $12.00. Mountain n' Air Books.

Cross Country Ski Vacations: A Guide to the Best Resorts, Lodges, and Groomed Trails in North America, Jonathan Wiesel, Dianna Delling. 1999. $15.95. John Muir Publications.

Ultimate Adventure Sourcebook, Paul McMenamin. 2000. $30.00. National Geographic. Great resource for all sorts of adventures, including Nordic skiing.

MAP & COMPASS

Be Expert with Map & Compass: The Complete Orienteering Handbook, Bjorn Kellstrom. U.S. Geological Survey & Orienteering Services. 1994. $17.00. Macmillan.

Compass & Map Navigator (rev): The Complete Guide to Staying Found, Michael Hodgson. 2000. $14.95. Globe Pequot Press. A guide for navigating through the wilds with or without a compass, with or without a map, and with all available tools including GPS.

Delorme Atlas/Gazetteers. Large-scale maps of most states with trails and campsites.

The Map Catalog, Joel Makower, ed. 1992. Out of print, but used copies are available for this classic. Vintage Books.

Map & Compass: The Basic Essentials, Cliff Jacobson. 2nd ed. 1999. $7.95. Globe Pequot Press.

Staying Found: The Complete Map & Compass Handbook, June Fleming. 3rd ed. 2001. $12.95. Mountaineers Books.

Trails Illustrated. A series published by a group of the same name, with topographical maps for major parks and mountains in the U.S.

VIDEOS

If you are without resources as far as instruction or guides, watching a video can reinforce the lessons in this book.

Trailside: Make Your Own Adventure
Our video series was originally broadcast on public television. *Trailside*'s Internet address is www.trailside.com. There you can order the books and videos, check out the *Trailside* trailer with RealVideo, and find station listings for the series. The following episodes present cross-country skiing experiences and related topics with tips and techniques presented by professionals. These videos and others in the *Trailside* series may be purchased by calling 1-800-TRAILSIDE (1-800-872-4574). A catalog is available.

Cross-Country Skiing in Northern Vermont. The frosty stillness of northern Vermont is broken only by the rhythmic swish of skis and the occasional bellow of a wild moose. (Order #713)

Cross-Country Skiing in Montana's Yellowstone Country. Discover one of the best-kept secrets in skiing: the cross-country ski trails of West Yellowstone, Montana. (Order #709)

Winter Adventure in Southern Utah's Canyon Country. Brian Head, Utah, offers incredible runs, virgin backcountry, and an average of over 400 inches per year of what's been called the greatest snow on earth. (Order #504)

Cross-Country Skiing the Grand Canyon's North Rim. Tips are offered on techniques about skiing on groomed and ungroomed backcountry trails. (Order #404)

And some other videos and films:

Free Time: Technique for Modern Freeheel Skiing. From Unparalleled Productions.

Freedom of the Heels. Covers the many aspects of backcountry skiing with lots of great footage.

High Velocity. The sport of biathlon combining the power-endurance of cross-country skiing with the focus of marksmanship. DVD and VHS versions available.

On Snow. Cross-country ski touring, racing, and training in Quebec and British Columbia. VHS.

Revenge of the Telemarkers. Sequel to the *Telemark Movie*, covers radical terrain techniques, mogul skiing, and more.

Tao of Skiing. Insight into the technical aspects of skiing with a focus on the way (Tao) in the correct preparation and execution of details.

Telemark Movie. Step-by-step instructional video on Telemark skiing techniques.

Telemark Workshop. Sequel to *Revenge of the Telemarkers,* covers hop turn, step-forward turn, step-back turn, and the Tele-roll.

Unparalleled. Digs to the roots of modern Telemark skiing and highlights some of today's most progressive riders. VHS.

Winning the Avalanche Game. Interviews with top avalanche professionals, shots of avalanches, route finding, equipment, and role of weather.

MAIL-ORDER/ON-LINE SOURCES OF BOOKS, MAPS, AND VIDEOS

For those of you far from a good bookstore, we recommend these fine suppliers.

Adventurous Traveler—www.adventuroustraveler.com—102 Lake Street, Burlington, VT 05401, 800-282-3963; over 10,000 books, maps, magazines, and gadgets for adventure travelers.

Amazon—www.amazon.com—the classic on-line source for new and used books as well as videos.

Booksense—www.booksense.com—recommendations from independent booksellers.

DeLorme Atlas/Gazetteers—www.delorme.com—Two DeLorme Drive, P.O. Box 298, Yarmouth, ME 04096, 800-511-2459 or 207-846-7000; detailed topographic maps for all fifty states; mapping software for GPS.

Garmin Map Source—www.gps4fun.com—Adventure GPS Products, 1629 Fourth Ave. S.E., Decatur, AL 35601, 888-477-4386 or 256-351-2151; international digital map source.

Powells—www.powells.com—on-line bookseller is an alternative to Amazon.

U.S. Geological Survey, P.O. Box 25286, Federal Center, Denver, CO 80225, 800-872-6277; current backcountry topographic maps.

Wilderness Press—www.wildernesspress.com—a source for outdoor books and maps.

XCZone—www.xczone.com—videos and DVDs on cross-country skiing.

MAIL-ORDER SOURCES OF EQUIPMENT

For those of you not lucky enough to live near an outfitter, the sources below can provide for all of your skiing needs.

CAMPMOR
P.O. Box 999
Paramus, NJ 07652
888-226-7667 or 201-445-5000
www.campmor.com
Campmor stocks everything from clothing to tents and sleeping bags. Also has a "virtual store."

CLIMB HIGH
2438 Shelburne Road
Shelburne, VT 05482
802-985-5055
www.climbhigh.com
E-mail:
info@climbhighretail.com
Full line of ski mountaineering equipment and clothing; specializes in rock- and ice-climbing gear.

EAGLE RIVER NORDIC
P.O. Box 936
Eagle River, WI 54521
800-423-9730 or 715-479-7285
www.ernordic.com
E-mail: ernordic@ernordic.com
Skating and classic skis, clothing, boots, and wax.

L.L.BEAN, INC.
Casco Street
Freeport, ME 04033
800-441-5713
www.llbean.com
The dean of outfitters, L.L.Bean is best known for quality clothing and camping gear at reasonable prices. It also carries a full line of cross-country skis and related gear.

MOUNTAIN TOOLS
P.O. Box 222295
Carmel, CA 93922
800-410-2514
www.mtntools.com
Full line of ski mountaineering equipment and clothing; specializes in rock- and ice-climbing gear.

NEW MOON SKI SHOP
P.O. Box 968
Hwy. 63 North
Hayward, WI 54843
800-754-8685 or 715-634-8685
www.newmoonski.com
Complete selection of cross-country gear, clothing, and accessories.

NORDICSKIIS
313 Elk Avenue
Crested Butte, CO 81224
866-349-1323 or 970-349-1323
www.nordicskiis.com
E-mail: dom@nordicskiis.com
Telemark, track, and backcountry touring gear.

PATAGONIA MAIL ORDER, INC.
8550 White Fir Street
P.O. Box 32050
Reno, NV 89523-2050
800-638-6464
www.patagonia.com
The finest in outdoor clothing.

REI—RECREATIONAL EQUIPMENT, INC.
Sumner, WA 98390
800-426-4840 or 253-891-2500
www.rei.com
Full line of skiing equipment and clothing.

RELIABLE RACING SUPPLY, INC.
643 Upper Glen Street
Queensbury, NY 12804
800-223-4448 or 518-793-5677
www.reliableracing.com
Full line of ski equipment and everything related.

SIERRA TRADING POST
5025 Campstool Road
Cheyenne, WY 82007
800-713-4534
www.sierratradingpost.com
Principally a vendor of apparel and footwear, but also features some snow sports gear.

SPORTS RACK
315 West Washington
Marquette, MI 49855
800-775-8338 or 906-225-1766
www.skiguys.com
Outstanding on-line Nordic service and equipment.

ACKNOWLEDGMENTS

I would like to offer my grateful appreciation to the following avalanche of people and organizations for making this project both rewarding and fun.

To my editor at W. W. Norton, John Barstow, whose guidance, thoughtfulness, and patience only made it seem as though this project went off without a glitch, my best wishes for a winter's worth of clear and plentiful Vermont powder. You've earned it.

To instructor and photographer par excellence Brian Litz, without whose timely direction I would still be veering into cybersnow, here's to a happy life of trail-breaking.

And for their invaluable contributions, my heartfelt thanks to the following: Deb Ackerman, Lara Bergel, Hartmut Buschbacher, Kendall Butz, Marko Cantor, Chris Frado, Steve Gaskill, Marc Groman, Laurie Gullion, The Holmenkollen Ski Museum, Tom Kelly, Tom Lohr, Chuck Lyda, Bob Kempainen, Bill Koch, Lyle Nelson, Gary Neptune, Paul Parker, Paul Peterson, Davis Phinney, The Professional Ski Instructors of America, Patty Ross, The Scandinavian Tourist Board, Casey Sheahan, Ski Industries America, Fred Taubman, Grete Waitz.

PHOTO CREDITS

BOB ALLEN: 17, 18, 20, 40, 44, 51, 56, 64, 84, 95 (all), 100, 107, 108

NANCIE BATTAGLIA: 15, 41, 66, 68, 135, 153, 157, 160, 167, 168, 174

ERIC EVANS: 127 (top)

JOHN GOODMAN: 32, 33 (4th from top), 34 (all), 37, 38, 43, 131, 151, 161

JOHN GOODMAN/COURTESY CLIMB HIGH: 22, 123, 128 (top), 129 (bottom), 141

JOHN GOODMAN/COURTESY KARHU: 29 (all)

JOHN GOODMAN/COURTESY ROSSIGNOL: 19, 28 (2nd, 3rd, 4th from left), 30, 33 (1st, 2nd from top)

STEVE HOWE: 39, 48, 70, 88, 122, 133, 140, 170

JOHN KELLY: 9, 11, 21, 54, 65, 81, 87, 97, 101, 102, 178

COURTESY L. L. BEAN: 28 (left), 33 (3rd from top), 127 (bottom), 128 (bottom), 129 (top)

BRIAN LITZ: 13, 35, 46, 49, 73, 82 (both), 83, 104, 106, 115 (all), 117, 118, 120, 121, 126, 130, 134, 138, 139, 148

BECKY LUIGART-STAYNER: 137

RON MACNEIL: 7, 10

TOM MORAN/SINGLETRACK: 158

JOEL W. ROGERS: 155

SCOTT SPIKER: 112

GORDON WILTSIE: 90, 111, 142, 164